EduKate Me II

A Survival Guide For the First Year Principal: Unspoken Commandments of School Leadership.

To Dr. Ott.
Success And
Happiness Always

E D   Y E R G A L O N I S

ISBN: 978-1-4834-1632-8 (sc)
ISBN: 978-1-4834-1631-1 (e)

Library of Congress Control Number: 2019909953

Lulu Publishing Services rev. date: 08/01/2019

Ten Unspoken Commandments of School Leadership

Foreword: Your leadership journey is about to begin.

1. Thou shalt always tell the truth—yet people do not want to hear the truth.
2. Thou shalt understand the importance of mental health because thou will be dealing with it.
3. Honor the politics of thy school. Understand that politics are everywhere and in everything.
4. Thou shalt strive for excellence when most people are very happy with mediocrity.
5. Thou shalt always ensure equity even though the system and people within the system may work against it.
6. Thou shalt know that thy knowledge is thine experience; thy graduate school education is useless.
7. Thou shalt lead with people and collaboration. Always understand that thy job is all about relationships.
8. Thou shalt know thyself. Always communicate what is important to thee.
9. Thou shalt use "the Force" to lead. Always understand that many people prefer the "dark side."
10. Thou shalt know thy job. Are thou an operations manager, or an instructional leader?

Afterword: They shoot horses, don't they? Everyone has a shelf life.

Foreword
Your Leadership Journey Is About to Begin

Ready, Set, Go

You have just accepted your first job as a school principal. This is the opportunity you have been waiting for. You feel that you have tirelessly prepared for this opportunity and are ready to accept the challenges that come with this new job. You have completed your graduate education and have been working your way up in the school hierarchy, and you are now looked upon as a true teacher leader. You tell yourself that you are ready for this.

Hold on a minute. I am about to burst your enthusiasm bubble because I am going to take you on a different type of journey. This journey is about reality. It is not about philosophy. It is not about textbook learning. It is about how you truly become a good principal. It is your real-life education. You will not be sitting in a classroom or taking any kind of formal test. But if you pay attention to the simple commandments I will present to you, I assure you that you will learn. It will not be an easy journey. Along the way, there will be numerous trials and tribulations, and in many cases, you will learn by failing, just like me. But if you have what it takes, you will be successful. You will not learn overnight. Becoming a principal takes perseverance and grit.

More importantly, I will show you that before you can *effectively lead, you must first learn how to survive.* This book is not about some glamorous strategic plan or the good things that you said in your interview. It is about the reality of being a school principal. It is about the reality of getting things done. That sounds so simple, but it is not. It is easy to fall into the trap of just spinning your wheels. It is personally defeating and demoralizing when you look back at the end of the week, the end of the month, or end of the year and find out that you have accomplished nothing. Please take my word for this because I have been there and done that. You will get to the point where you measure your success by just making it through the day. There were days when I was happy to make it through my school's lunchtime incident free because a bad day in the cafeteria can wreck your day and maybe your week. This is no way to lead. You are surviving at the simplest level. If you know how to survive, you will have a better chance to lead.

This book is about the things no one ever told you about. They are all things that will quickly sink your principalship if you are not prepared. Although I explain my journey through a series of scenarios, the book is really not about the scenarios per se. The book is about my reaction to these scenarios *and more importantly, the mistakes I made in reacting to these scenarios.*

I know that we won't always agree on how I handled these situations. As a matter of fact, I hope that we do not agree. With hindsight, I would have done many things differently. But if this book causes you to think about the role of the principal, I will consider it a great success. And if you internalize what I have to say, I think that you will end up becoming a successful and effective principal.

So the story begins here. I was an educator for almost thirty-nine years. I believe once you are a teacher, you are always a teacher. Some principals forget that. Some who ascend to the principal's office immediately forget where they came from. When you become a principal, it is critical that you still consider yourself a teacher. You must never stop teaching. You now become not only a teacher of your students, but you are also now a teacher of your teachers and any other person in your school. You must remain a teacher first. Maybe that is your first lesson: you are always a teacher, always a coach.

Some people only want to become a principal to escape the classroom. This is a sad indictment of our profession.

This journey I will take you on has many twists and turns. Some detours will seem insurmountable. Some scenarios I present to you are almost impossible to believe. It is these detours that we will examine. We will examine my response to these detours. Yes, you can be that Monday-morning quarterback. You can be that after-dinner speaker. I know that I am undefeated as a Monday-morning quarterback. Your experience with this book will only be successful if you pause, reflect, and think about what you would have done.

You must always be in the moment. Looking back and second guessing yourself are wasted activities. Of course, you must learn from each situation and once you mentally debrief, move on. Try not to dwell on past events. You cannot bring them back. As I tell my stories, I will not use any names and may have slightly altered situations to try to ensure anonymity. *Remember that purpose of this book is to evaluate my response or my observations, not the overall situation.*

I remain personally indebted to all of my colleagues I have worked with over the years and all of the thousands of students I have had the honor of serving. Teaching remains a noble profession. I am forever glad that I made this my lifetime choice.

Commandment 1
Thou Shalt Always Tell the Truth—Yet People Really Never Want to Hear the Truth

Do You Swear to Tell the Whole Truth and Nothing but the Truth?

Now that is an interesting question. If this oath were part of your employment contract, you would quickly be fired. The reality in a school is that it is very hard to tell the truth. I have found that most school cultures have been built to make the adults feel good rather than to improve performance. With both students and teachers, we have substituted feel-good initiatives for achievement initiatives. This is why many schools continue to underperform.

I find it somewhat comical when teachers clamor for honesty and transparency from a principal, but the minute you exercise that candor with that individual, all of a sudden, there is no longer that need or desire for honesty. People want you to be honest with everyone else but not necessarily with them.

I am convinced that until we can have that candid—and yes, crucial—conversation with ease in our schools, true improvement will be hard to see. And yes, I believe that principals are responsible for this. *We readily sacrifice the truth for expediency.* We must continue to attempt to build the culture of our schools around the truth. Feedback is not personal. People need to realize that negative feedback does not mean that you do not like them. You are attempting to help them grow. It sounds so simple, but it rarely is.

Leadership Lessons Learned

- *People do not really want to hear the truth.* They will clamor for honesty and transparency—for everyone but themselves.
- *Never sacrifice the truth for expediency.* You will wrestle with this concept on a daily basis. Fight hard to resist this temptation.

Not My Finest Hour

You will get to the point when you will look back at your career and be able to see things with great clarity and honesty. You will see things that you did well, and you will see the things that you did not do so well. I know I tend to be overly critical of myself, but that is my nature. *I am never satisfied.* At the end of the day, I think that is an admirable quality, a quality found in many successful leaders.

I am rarely considered an enabler. I tend to be more confrontational. If you do not believe me, go ask my children. However, in the situation I am about to describe, I enabled and lived to regret it. The responsibility for this travesty lay squarely upon my shoulders.

I walked into the classroom for an unannounced classroom observation of a teacher. I saw the room essentially divided in half. Although there was no line of demarcation on the floor, there could have been. For the ten to fifteen students behind the line, it was a very social experience. Some were doing their nails, chatting, reading magazines, or sleeping. The students in front of the line were paying attention to the teacher, who was at the board. Was I in one of my classrooms or some sort of imaginary dream? Did I enter the twilight zone?

It took me a few minutes to understand what was going on. I asked the teacher to pause and see me in the hallway.

I listened intently as the teacher explained that only those students who wanted to learn would be taught. The others could do what they pleased as long as they did not bother the learners. After all, these students were in high school, and they could make these choices.

I told the teacher to clean up this mess and I would come back to do another observation. I gave this teacher a do-over.

I returned on another day; I even picked a different period for the new observation. When I gave the teacher a do-over, I really gave this teacher a career do-over.

My response to this ineffective teaching was probably as grossly negligent as the teaching. I enabled poor teaching to continue.

I should have helped organize the class, which would have allowed all students to be taught. I also should have written the observation as it happened and after that provided a network of support to coach this teacher. This was an experienced teacher who should have been able to effectively teach all students and control the class.

I probably did everything but help this teacher improve his or her teaching. A constructive improvement plan should have been implemented at once and closely monitored. Ultimately, other incidents occurred. I never addressed the real problem.

I look back at this as one of my biggest mistakes in the supervision of staff. But why did this happen? This is the lesson that you must learn as a new principal. The teacher was a nice person, cooperative, well-presented, never a complainer, and a team player. The instructor was well liked by the staff, parents, and students. If you needed a chaperone at an event, this teacher was there. I accepted all of that peripheral stuff. I neglected teaching and learning. I cheated every student who came into contact with this teacher. Don't let this happen to you. *Do your job!*

Leadership Lessons Learned

- *You can never ignore poor teaching.* Nice people who are bad teachers cannot slip through the cracks. You have to call it as you see it. *Never close an eye to anything. If you do, it will come back to haunt you!* Things do not get better when you ignore them. You cannot survive ineffective teachers by allowing do-overs!
- *People need and deserve fair and honest feedback.* Leaders need professional development on giving feedback, and everyone needs professional development on receiving feedback. You must be proactive.
- *Giving feedback is all about evidence.* For each piece of feedback you give a person, you must show the accompanying evidence. If you do not provide this evidence, people may feel like you are making random statements and may be out to get them.
- *Personal relationships cannot cloud your feedback.* You cannot get too friendly with those whom you supervise because one day you may have to be honest!
- *You must forever be the coach.* Coach your people up, and do it right.

Better Late Than Never. Oh Really?

Let's take a moment to think about that. Is it better to be late in doing something or not to do it at all? I guess your answer depends on the situation. In some cases, it is critical that you complete a task regardless of any imposed timeline, so yes, it is better that you were late. In other cases, it just doesn't matter. But what about when it comes to renewing a teacher or letting that teacher go? In that case, it is always better to be late. Let that teacher go before any sort of tenure is earned.

Let's not kid ourselves. Although rules have relaxed a bit, if you let an ineffective teacher gain tenure, it is too late.

Some teaching positions are just about impossible to fill. I used to become almost physically ill when I had to seek a chemistry, mathematics, or special education teacher. You cannot let the idea of the difficulty in filling these positions cloud your decision-making with regard to keeping a subpar teacher. I did.

I had a teacher who was struggling teaching in one of the aforementioned areas. There was never a doubt that the teacher lacked class management skills. Most days you could see this by merely walking by the classroom. But content knowledge was never an issue. The teacher knew the curriculum. I also thought the teacher had the pedagogical skills to be successful. However, the teacher could not manage the class. And these were our top, most focused learners. I think the students liked the teacher because they were never really pushed and were always given good grades. The parents were happy. They did not seem to care if anything was learned as long as their child got a high grade. Suffice to say, this teacher was ineffective. Yet I always gave the teacher satisfactory evaluations because once again, just as we saw in the previous scenario, this person was nice. Also because of the inflated grades, high-maintenance parents stayed out of the principal's office. And let's not kid ourselves: we never want to see that high-maintenance parent in our office!

Ultimately, in the final evaluation before tenure, a decision was made not to renew this teacher. One small problem: the teacher never had any documented deficiencies in any performance review. This teacher never had a clue that this was a nonrenewal. We made matters worse by delivering the bad news by merely placing the nonrenewal evaluation in a sealed envelope in the teacher's mailbox. Shame on us!

Going forward, this procedure was corrected for the entire district. All evaluations had to be personally hand-delivered so that a meeting could be mutually scheduled to discuss the evaluation after it was privately reviewed. There could also be no surprises. No one should ever be surprised when he or she is let go. If you are doing your job correctly, this will never happen. And each evaluation should contain evidence of what was unsatisfactory. Then effective corrective plans need to be implemented

Needless to say, the teacher was disappointed. Perhaps the person was more disappointed in me and the way it was handled than the actual outcome. I own that. I believe the teacher knew that this teacher/school partnership was not a good fit.

The teacher did not fight the nonrenewal, but the points that were shared with me were certainly credible. My entire leadership team blew it. Try sitting in that meeting with nothing but egg on your face.

I can assure you that I learned a great deal from this scenario, and it never repeated itself. I personally grew from this, and those I supervised grew with me.

And yes, no matter how difficult this was, it was better to let this person go, albeit late.

Leadership Lessons Learned

- *You must confront subpar performance.* I tried to kick the can down the road. I knew in my heart that this teacher was not going to make it long-term, and I let the situation play out for a full three years. This was unacceptable.
- *Don't put off until tomorrow what you can do today.* When you know something needs to get done, do it. If you continue to wait for the right time, that time will never come.
- *Get your head out of the sand.* This teacher was not going to miraculously improve without assistance.
- *There should never be any surprises when it comes to performance appraisals.* People should always know where they stand, and this must be provided in writing. A person never should be surprised when it comes to a nonrenewal. You must have evidence, evidence, and more evidence.

To Lead or to Bully? That Is the Question.

Are you a good principal, or are you just a big bully? I hate to say it, but I feel that many school leaders are nothing more than big bullies, and the higher up in the chain of command that you go, the bigger bully you become. Perhaps this observation is more related to the notion that the further you get away from people, the easier it is to lose track of the grassroots people.

I can speak from experience on that one. When I became the superintendent, it was much easier for me to be curt, authoritarian, and directive. It was a not a conscious action, but I knew it happened. I did not have to work day in and day out in a school with the same staff. Never lose track of your roots. Know where you came from.

I worked for a period of time with a superintendent who was a masterful change agent. He came into the district and disrupted everything. I forged a good relationship with him, and he tried to mentor me. He told me that he would come into a district and throw all the balls up in the air. Those that stuck would be a lasting, positive change to the district. He also knew that because of his style, he would never last too long in one district, and when he left, the district would be in a better place.

One day he summoned me to his office to serve as a witness to a meeting he was to have with another administrator. Everyone arrived, and after some brief pleasantries were exchanged, he lambasted my colleague. The attack was brutal. It was an onslaught. I had never seen anything like it. I tried to hide. If I would have been able to crawl under the couch that we were sitting on, I would have. I shrank up and tried to be invisible.

My colleague did not become flustered and used active listening skills to break the momentum. On the surface, this administrator held up fine. I never asked how he or she felt on the inside. I know that I would have probably broken down and cried. I think I am mentally tough, but I do not think I could have survived this tongue lashing. I would have emotionally cracked.

When he was done, he dismissed this person but asked me to wait around. I thought I was going to be next in line for some reason. He just wanted to make sure that "I got it." The only thing I got during this meeting was to learn what not to do. It is a behavior that I think I never replicated. This was not me. That is not to suggest that I never got upset with someone and perhaps I got close to his performance a couple of times, but I swore to myself that I would never handle a situation like that. I could do better.

Leadership Lessons Learned

- *The relationships that you cultivate at work must be based on respect, not fear or intimidation.*
- *You must stay true to your vision.* There will be times when you have setbacks on your personal journey. Yet if you remain true to yourself, you will be able to put your head peacefully down on the pillow at night.
- *Change agents do not last in a district.* If you see yourself as this change agent, it is important to fully understand that. Your style and behavior will wear people out.

You May Not Get a Second Chance

Sometimes you wake up and wonder if your decisions matter. I know that since I have retired from active school supervision, the one thing that I cherish is that I do not have to make any more decisions. It was a tremendous burden off of my back. I especially welcomed joining this no decision-making zone when the snow started falling for the first time. I did not have to decide if school was opened, closed, or operating on some sort of delay. It sometimes sounds so trite, but it is one of the many critical decisions for staff, students, and all of your families. Suffice it to say, your decisions matter and sometimes your decisions have a far-reaching and great magnitude. And sometimes you do not get that second chance.

You never need a crisis to start the year, but nonetheless, no matter how much you hope, you can never predict when a crisis will arrive on your doorstep

It was the first day of school, and we were welcoming the entire student body of approximately fifteen hundred students, over a hundred teachers, and a full assortment of support personnel. My administrative team was ready. We were prepared. And then my phone rang. The call was from the county sheriff's office explaining that our school, along with several others in the county, was the recipient of what their intelligence viewed as a credible bomb threat. The law at the time left it entirely up to me if we were to evacuate.

It was not many years after 9/11, and if the sheriff thought the threat was credible, I was not going to take any chances. We quickly evacuated the building.

I thought chaos would ensue. I was wrong. Everyone rose to the challenge. The county police department brought their trained bomb-sniffing dogs to do a sweep of the building. The dogs came, did their job, indicated all was safe to return, and left. (As an aside, I was allowed to watch the dogs work. It is amazing how quickly they can do their jobs.) We were probably outside of the building for about forty-five minutes. Obviously, we never found that bomb, but what if we did? I am sure that the principals who have experienced an active shooter never thought that it could happen to them, but it did. This sheds some light on the importance of taking all of your emergency drills seriously and communicating that seriousness to everyone in the school. You never know when it can happen to you. Never let your guard down. Never become complacent in this regard.

You must always work to nurture your relationship with the local police agencies. They need to be your friends so that when you call, because of your strong relationship, they respond quickly and in full force. Likewise, when they called me, I responded with a seriousness of purpose. I was extremely proud of how my staff and students responded on that day. You will not be able to say that on all days. I was extremely proud of our municipal and county law enforcement officers on that day. Everyone did a great job. Not a single person let me down.

Leadership Lessons Learned

- *Make sure that your relationships with all local law enforcement agencies are positive and collegial.* It is easy to engage in turf wars, but I assure you that if you play this game with your local police, you will lose. You must be open and honest.

- *Always take your drills seriously, and when people get it right, show some gratitude.*

Shame, Shame, Shame. Shame on You!

For years, one of our local television news programs did a weekly expose on some unscrupulous contractor or confused bureaucrat. I can almost hear the jingle in my head. I would have parents threaten to call the local news every time they were not happy. Usually the news stations ignored it, but every now and then a news truck would end up in front of my school looking for some crazy story. Never forget that in most cases, the news is trying to make your school or you personally look bad.

We were warned that a reporter would be looking to do an expose about how our school opened. A reporter decided to pose as a new student in an undercover operation. This reporter was looking to see how easily a stranger could enter the building and how inefficient our staff was in finding someone who did not belong. It did not help that we were a transient community where there was a continual stream of students in and out of the school.

Remember that the press is looking to sell newspapers. This type of expose keeps their readers interested. I have a great deal of respect for the press and understand the job they do.

Early in my career, I trusted too many reporters and was burned several times. After that I worked hard to build a very strong and honest relationships with the press.

Since we had a hunch this was going to happen, we spent a great deal of time preparing for the event. We communicated this to our staff, and we were all on the same page about what to do. Although we always had the plan, we accentuated it because we knew trouble was coming.

This time good luck was with us. I am also happy to say that within minutes of the homeroom period, we had apprehended the young reporter who could easily pass as a student. This occurred because of our preparation and the heads-up action of our staff. We had the police join us because he was clearly a trespasser. Although we never pressed charges, he left us in shame, and more importantly, we never saw a derogatory story on this topic. And we were not the ones shamed. I always wondered and still wonder to this day why we never saw a story about how good our entry procedures were. Of course, I know why this did not happen. Good news just won't sell newspapers!

Leadership Lessons Learned

- *Cultivate and nurture a positive and strong relationship with your local press.* It will pay dividends for you in the long run. Always call them back. Even if you have no comment, give them the courtesy of a return phone call.
- *Know that in any of these situations, your staff can sabotage you along the way.* Some of your malcontents would love to see the school and you smeared. Work to minimize the chance of this happening. Being honest with them and showing gratitude are good places to start.

Digging Deeper into Honesty and Telling the Truth

Sometimes we just have to dig a little deeper. At the conclusion of each chapter we will dig a little deeper into the leadership element discussed in the chapter. These will be additional snippets that I ask you to reflect upon.

Leadership Lessons Learned

- *You must nurture your talent.* Support them and hold high expectations. Then, you must help them attain your lofty goals.
- *Your teachers must realize that becoming a master teacher is hard work and takes time.* You become a good teacher by being a teacher, listening to feedback, and tirelessly working on your craft. You

become a good principal in the same way. It sounds so simple. Then why do we make it so difficult? A new teacher must know that this is long journey.

- *Stop creating more widgets.* We have now lived through the evaluation revolution and are stuck with a variety of systems probably no better than the ones we discarded. At one time we evaluated everyone as satisfactory. Now everyone is effective.

- *You must possess and hone your skill set to be an effective coach.* Some principals may pass everyone through as effective because they do not possess the skill set to effectively evaluate. *You cannot coach what you do not know. It just doesn't work.*

- There will be times when you will not be recommending a colleague, maybe a close professional friend, for a promotion. *Always tell a person directly with a face-to- face conversation.* He or she cannot hear about your recommendation through the rumor mill.

- *Work to make sure that the interview process is legitimate and not rigged.* The process cannot be just a ruse so you can appoint someone from the old boys network. I have been through many of these interviews sitting on the other side of the table where I knew that the candidate was already selected. Don't waste everyone's time.

Commandment 2
Thou Shalt Understand the Importance of Mental Health Because Thou Will Be Dealing with It.

Welcome to the Ship of Fools; You Are Not an Educator, You Are a Psychiatrist

In 1962, Katherine Ann Porter published the novel *Ship of Fools*. It is a complex allegory dealing with the quest for Utopia and the concept of eternity. In 1965, the novel was made into an Academy Award–winning movie. I do not recall how I happened to find this novel, but the work became a personal metaphor for my school at times. In these moments I thought that I was the captain of this ship navigating all on board on a very special and perhaps bizarre journey.

People become teachers for a variety of reasons. You would hope that everyone becomes a teacher for the right reason, but I can assure you that is untrue. Some choose this field for power or convenience. Some choose it because they need some free therapy and their students will serve as built-in captive therapists. Group therapy is held every period of the day. I have seen my share of crying, ranting and raving, and withdrawal. Some people need this mental and emotional therapy every day. You must learn quickly that you cannot be their therapist, so do not even try. You cannot allow your students to be subjected to this behavior. If you do, you are cheating them. You can be supportive and caring, but never forget *that some people are just crazy.*

Leadership Lessons Learned

- *Never forget that you are an educator, not a psychiatrist or counselor.* Stay in your lane.
- *You may never figure out the motivation of some people, so stop trying.* Some people are just not rational or sane. You can never let this impact your students. It is hard not to.

Handcuffs, a Whip, and Edible Undies, Oh My!

I could almost see it coming. I saw the dynamics change. I saw a more casual tone. I began to see a bit of a cliquish nature develop. I saw the identity of this office begin to change. People started to let their hair down—perhaps too much. The line between the adults and the students was getting blurred. Upon reflection, it came from the leadership in this office—or lack thereof. We were headed down a dangerous road. We were on a slippery slope. Looking back, I knew trouble was brewing, but how bad could it be? Perhaps I did not act quickly enough to change this new culture because I had just left the building for my new role of assistant superintendent for the district and was personally caught up in this transition. My head was not there, and perhaps it should have been. Who knows?

Nonetheless, building administration should have seen it coming. Let me set the stage. The attendance office in this high school tended to be one of the busiest places in the school. It was always a hotbed for activity. Students were constantly coming and going, parents were always present, and there was always a need for the faculty to be there handing in a class cut slip or disciplinary referral or checking on a student's attendance. The office operated from 7:00 a.m. until 4:00 p.m., with rarely, if ever, a quiet time. It was managed by an assistant principal who had an office on one side of the large former classroom, and at the other end of the office was another adult in a quasi-administrative role serving as a coordinator of student management, known more commonly as a dean of students. A great deal of disciplinary issues came out of this office. Two secretaries supported the process, and teachers were assigned there on a by- period basis to help and to make calls home to absent students. It was also a location that our three safety officers came to call home. From an outsider's viewpoint, it could have been seen as organized chaos. I know this well because I started my administrative career there and spent almost eight years in charge of this area. For me, this office was my home.

One day I was hurriedly dispatched to this office by a phone call, and the voice on the other end of the phone told me that when I got there, "I would not believe my eyes." Sure enough, upon my arrival, I knew that they were correct. Sitting out in the open in plain sight on the counter was a brightly adorned gift basket. It looked like a basket wrapped for a tricky tray type of fundraiser or a well-decorated Easter basket. Yet the contents of this basket were explicit sexually related material, including a XXX DVD, edible underwear, handcuffs, a whip, some bondage items, and other general adult-only types of toys. I think you get the picture. Obviously, we had the basket removed and confiscated at once and began our investigation of what the hell was going on.

Several of my safety officers, along with one of the secretaries in the office, decided to do some of their own personal fundraising. They were selling raffle tickets to win this basket in a drawing. They claimed they never sold tickets to a student. I sincerely doubt that. The students loved these individuals in part because at times they operated on the same maturity level. Remember that the lines of authority in this office became quite blurred. The adults involved saw nothing wrong with this activity and were amazed at how upset I became.

To my astonishment, the vice principal who was in charge of this this office knew about it and by his silence approved of it. They never asked his permission, but once he saw it, he should have acted upon it immediately. He actually purchased a ticket. Talk about the lack of common sense and administrative overall immaturity. As a result of this situation, all parties involved either resigned or were terminated. Yet as a result of this escapade, the office and the school suffered a big hit to its credibility.

Who could dream up this sort of scheme? And what potential principal would ever think that they would have to deal with it?

In today's era of workplace sexual harassment, another layer of issues is added to your plate as the principal. Issues that might have been ignored, condoned, or laughed at in the past must now be handled immediately. And you will find that in most cases bringing any sort of closure to these issues is extremely difficult, time consuming, and energy draining.

Leadership Lessons Learned

- *Make sure that everyone knows your expectations of behavior.* These folks lacked judgment and common sense. After the incident, I decided to put a script together highlighting many of the cases you see in this book. New hires had to sign an annotated summary of this speech. It was an action I needed to take in response to this lunacy.
- *Dedicate enough time to on-board staff effectively.*
- *The most important leadership lesson to be learned from this scenario was that we allowed a subculture to develop within the school.* The attendance office became an unmonitored location where the climate took on a life of its own. It became too relaxed, too informal, and too casual.

The Case of the Wily Whistler

I had a little mystery on my hands, and yes, I did feel a bit like Perry Mason. Solving my mystery proved as difficult as one of Mason's many cases. Perry Mason never lost. Did I win, or did I lose? On this one, I think I lost.

I can remember walking down the halls and hearing a blaring gym teacher type of whistle being blown in the hallway. The first time that I heard this sound, I started to look for the student who was doing this. When I could not find a student culprit, I started to think it was one of my gym teachers implementing a new and bizarre method of monitoring the hallways. I was now on a mission, and once I went on one of my missions, I became relentless.

At about the same time the mystery whistler made a first appearance, an experienced teacher began to accuse several of the teachers in the building of sexual harassment. I investigated the complaints and could never corroborate any of the accusations. As time progressed, the stories became more outlandish and more bizarre. Thankfully, there was never a claim of any physical touching. The claims always focused on a form of stalking. There was also a claim that one of my teachers was following this person home. This individual now focused on this staff member and became obsessed. A police report was made, but the police also could not substantiate any of the claims. I spent a great deal of time and effort investigating the claims. I followed the accused, I stationed myself in the hallway by the class, and I was in the parking lot when teachers departed. I found nothing out of the ordinary. I interviewed both parties. I attempted to find witnesses and interviewed them. I offered to bring the parties together to mediate this situation. The accuser declined my offer. I asked the association leadership for help, and now everyone was getting their own personal lawyer to handle it. At year's end, the accused retired and the accuser soon left the district.

I am sure that you have guessed by now that the accuser was my wily whistler. This person started to wear a gym whistle on a lanyard and would blow the whistle loudly when they were near the suspect. It was crazy and lasted for months.

Leadership Lessons Learned

- *You must remain impartial.* I think I became overly sensitive to the allegation of sexual harassment and being accused of allowing a hostile work environment to exist. These are hot-button items. Because of this concern, I gave the accuser the benefit of doubt.
- *Crucial conversations are essential.* This was not normal behavior, and I should have been stronger in addressing it. People whispered behind the accuser's back about the perceived instability. *I should*

have been stronger in confronting the accuser. Experience will help mold you. I never let this type of situation happen again.

I Want to Run; I Want to Hide

Unlike the 1987 U2 song "Where the Streets Have No Name," this story is not about tearing down walls; it is about building walls. It is about how a teacher tried to isolate himself from his students. Instead of building relationships with his students, he sought to ignore them. Perhaps he felt that if he ignored them long enough, they would just go away. This is also a story of a teacher who once had it but lost it and did not know what to do about it.

This teacher was once a proud educator. He was challenging, demanding, and fun. The students and parents liked him. He knew his content and made it come alive.

Time just caught up with him. Unfortunately, this was my first principalship, and I did not know how to handle his deterioration. Maybe I just did not see the signs or, maybe if I saw the signs, I did not know what to do about it. Other adults in the building saw the same thing. But instead of doing something about it, we collectively just stuck our heads in the sand.

Over time he gradually began stacking books up around the perimeter of his desk. Gradually, the stack grew so high that you could no longer see the teacher when he sat down. He was a short man to begin with, and he was actually able to physically hide from the students in his own classroom. He built a fortress. Instead of building bridges, he built walls. If it wasn't so sad, it would have been comical. You actually could not see him from any seat in the classroom. And surprisingly, the students never misbehaved. I think somehow, they intuitively knew his condition and made an unwritten pact not to bother him. He handed out worksheets or read to the students. It was not a challenging academic environment.

At around the same time, I started to receive phone calls from this teacher at home very late in the night. I could not even understand what he was saying. His speech was confused and unintelligible. What the heck was going on? More importantly, what should I have done about it?

Believe it or not, for a while, I did nothing about it. I spoke to him about the calls, and he shared with me that he was a diabetic and sometimes his insulin situation would be off, so he attributed these calls to this. The school nurse confirmed that this was a possibility, so we explored other potential scenarios. As far as his stacking of books was concerned, he claimed he did not know he was doing this and would stop. He did stop for a while, but the stacks soon returned. I allowed him to dance with me throughout the entire year. He started the next year off in the same manner but soon retired. Not many years after this, he quietly died.

I knew what was wrong with him, but I did not have the skill set to address it. Deep down, I knew he was an alcoholic and his teaching skills were so eroded that I needed to remove him from the classroom and get him some help. He should not have been around students. After he retired, some of the veteran teachers confirmed my suspicion that he was a well-known alcoholic for a long time. His diabetes just compounded the negative issues. If our school culture was a bit better, maybe the veteran staff would have shared this with me. Understand that building trust takes time.

But handling this situation was my responsibility. I was the principal. I was never direct and honest with him. I should have stopped the process and required a full physical and complete screening for drugs and alcohol. I had the power within the contract to do that, but I did not. The district had plenty of resources to help this individual. I also should have reached out to the association leadership for assistance. By allowing this situation to linger, I cheated many students. I never let this happen again.

Leadership Lessons Learned

- *No matter what the reason, you cannot allow physically or mentally ill or ineffective teachers to stay in the classroom.* Either help them or remove them.

- *Trust your instincts.* They are probably correct.
- *Seek assistance.* When you are traveling down a new road, it is acceptable to ask for help. Handling things alone ineffectively does not make you a good leader. Perhaps the exact opposite occurs. Good leaders know when to reach out for help. They know when they are in over their heads.

Sex in the City

In all likelihood, you will have to deal with an inappropriate relationship between a student and a teacher. If you suspect something, pick up the phone and report it to your area's child protection agency, along with your local police department. Do not wait. You cannot let this slip through the cracks.

One day I was summoned to the office via my walkie-talkie (standard issue for a school administrator). A student was there to see me. I did not want to see this student or anyone at the moment. I had a sea of paperwork to do, and I had etched out this time in my schedule to attempt to do it. Nonetheless, I reluctantly saw the student, hoping it would be quick.

I knew the student, and I suspected that there would be some drama involved. However, without any small talk, the student directly asked when it became acceptable for teachers to have sex with their students. I was dumbfounded. I felt like I just got hit over the head by a two- by-four and thought selfishly, *There goes my paperwork.* She told me more of the details of what led her to believe that was true, and apparently, it was pretty much common knowledge among her peer group. Where the hell was I? How come it seemed like I was the last to know? I believed this young lady. I forced myself to resist the temptation to dismiss this claim as merely the usual drama from this student.

I stopped what I was doing and immediately picked up the phone and called the state's child protection agency and reported the story. They took the report seriously, and within a day, they were in my building investigating and conducting all the needed interviews. The local police were quickly called into the case, and you by now know where this story is headed. Of course, the allegation was proven to be true. The staff member was engaged in a sexual affair with one of the students. I do not need to go into all of the details. It is enough that you know that it was true. The teacher was suspended and ultimately terminated. As part of a plea agreement with the courts, her teacher's license was permanently revoked. No jail time was ever served.

Leadership Lessons Learned

- *Turn information like this immediately over to the appropriate authorities.* You are not the investigator. You must work with them and be supportive, but let them do the investigation. What would have happened if I ignored the student? How badly could this student or subsequent students been hurt? It also could have been a career ending mistake for me. I also think that my credibility rose with the students and the staff as result of how I handled this issue.
- *Never assume, apply stereotypes or believe in preconceived notions.*
- *When you hire someone, always review what constitutes an appropriate adult student relationship.* Be candid and specific. As hard as it may be to believe, some people do not get it.
- *Always nurture your resource pipeline.* You need to know everything that happens in your building. Students and staff hear more than you do, and they need to share this with you.
- *Document, document, and document some more.* Do not forget any of the details. You will be hurt by sloppy note taking.

Digging Deeper into the Issue of Mental Health

Leadership Lessons Learned

- One time I had to confront a situation where the teacher refused to take the gym class outside for instruction because she was fearful of the radioactive cloud that was over Russia after Chernobyl, a significant nuclear accident. This teacher was sent to me as part to the "dance of the lemons." You know that little dance administrators do where they pass ineffective teachers between buildings, hoping to force a resignation or retirement. It was now my turn. It was a long year with this person. Remember that *you cannot cure mental illness. You must deal with it.* You must get the person out of the classroom as soon as possible. You cannot run the risk of someone being hurt by one person's craziness. And this person was crazy! This was a long time coming, and the district, instead of passing her around, should have made her deal with her condition.

- In another situation I had to deal with a paraprofessional who ended up having a fistfight with a student on a weekend off site. This employee thought it was fine because it was not on school property or on school time. I hold the belief that you work in a school twenty-four hours a day. seven days a week. Your behavior follows you. Is this fair? I do not know, but for me you always need to be that role model.

- *You can never assume that all people know what doing the right thing means.* You must be explicit when you hire staff. You must try to do the impossible—namely, tell them everything they need to know because the one thing that you leave out, you will be forced to deal with.

- *Hire the right person.* Many times principals will rush the process, especially involving support personnel. I contend that instead of taking less time, you need to put more time into the process. Problems with support staff will kill you.

Commandment 3
Honor the Politics of Thy School. Understand That Politics Are Everywhere and in Everything.

You Are a Big Boy (or Girl) Now

Like it or not, you have entered the world of grown-ups. I am always amazed when I speak with a new principal and see how naïve they are. I encourage you to check your naivete at the door because you have entered perhaps one of the most political entities that exists: a school district.

Would you accuse me of being cynical if I told you that from the minute you enter the world of administration, politics will push or pull you in a specific direction? In most districts, it is always about the politics. I would be extremely surprised if you got your appointment to administration solely based upon your merit. I could forensically analyze each appointment and probably see some political strand that runs through it.

That being said, your tenure and survival in this position will be based in part as to how well that you play this game. There will be a time when you will have to sacrifice what you may believe to keep the political machine moving in what you think is the right direction. You may think that you will be above it all, but if you truly intend to stay above it, you may be looking for a job every several years. I think the key to surviving this political monster is to know that like so many other things, it is more or less an ebb-and-flow phenomenon. I caution you and perhaps encourage you that at times, you may have to bend, but do not break. Never do anything illegal or against your professional ethics. The job is not worth it.

You will see politics at work in every aspect of your job. These are especially prevalent in hiring and job assignments. These areas are ripe for the local power brokers.

Leadership Lessons Learned

- *Politics are everywhere.* Each school district is unique.
- *Bend but never break.* The extent of the politics in your district will probably ebb and flow depending upon the situation. Never do anything illegal. You may be tested.
- *The greatest pressure you will feel comes regarding hiring and job assignments.* Every politician wants to act like the godfather of the community. They want to hold people hostage by doing favors for them. Always look for ulterior motives when you get that phone call regarding these topics.

I Got the Power! Baby, Baby, Baby, I Got the Power!

Why do people want to become board of education members? I was very fortunate to come into contact with some wonderful people who possessed a very simple agenda. They wanted to better the education of the children in the community. These positions were volunteer positions, and these individuals committed hours and hours of personal time. For these people, their only expectation of payment was being part of the achievement and growth of the young people in the community. At times, I thought these people were rare.

Many people I worked with on the board of education operated with a specific personal agenda. They had a mission for themselves or a small constituency of voters. Being a board member can be a thankless job.

Some of these people just wanted to matter. They wanted to be important. They wanted to be a "somebody" in the community. Many were uneducated and unqualified. They did not want to learn how to be a board member. They just wanted action—their action!

Some would seek to become a board member because they had an ax to grind or wanted to pave the way for a family member or friend. Although stronger ethics laws have worked to tighten these rules, people have skillfully learned to work around them. They were there to get jobs for friends and family.

Each year, after election day, the chemistry of the board changes. One new person can cause a drastic change. So every year, new norms had to be set. It would be great if the board recognized this and talked about the norms and the way they should operate. These conversations rarely happened. Retreats were scheduled and canceled. They just did not feel it was important. This was not what they cared about.

Some of these individuals just wanted to boss other people around. They would attempt to push you around in a variety of ways. They became bullies. They would wear you down with incessant phone calls and demands.

When one of my board members needed to discuss something with me, he would ask me to meet him. He would jump in my car and tell me to drive. Most often, we just drove around town. He talked. I listened. I always sensed a big request was coming. I used to wonder if this person would stay up nights thinking about things to task me with. He was an idea generator. I do not think he was ever looking to professionally or personally hurt me. A matter of fact, we actually liked one another. One time he told me that he just wanted to help me. I did attempt to share, without being hurtful, that I really did not need his help. I never thought he got it.

One time I felt pressure from the local municipal politicians for the school district to purchase a piece of vacant real estate in the town. They presented a strong, united push for me to enter into a lease for this vacant piece of property. Yes, we could use the property, but we could never afford it. Additionally, if we did lease the space, we would have to build it out to a tune of several million dollars more. We did not have the money. The group of politicians had already identified what I could use the space for. I am glad they knew my job better than me. You will find that many people in the community view your job, whether it is a principal position or the superintendent position, as an easy job that they could do much better than you. It did not matter if they were educated or had any experience. In their eyes, your job was easy.

I wanted to thank the group and run away because I knew another shoe was about to fall. They then brought up some creative ways to finance this project that made no sense to me.

Ultimately, I explained that I could not enter into this deal. We did not have the funding. I do not think that they cared. To this very day, I know that some people of the group hold my reluctance and reticence against me. Who cares? I did the right thing.

Leadership Lessons Learned

- *Know that when you work with a board of education, you may have multiple hidden agendas operating.* Do what is right for the students!
- *Power can corrupt as it changes people.*
- *Some people just need to matter.* Never forget that some people gain their self-identity through their perceived power.
- *Beware of strangers bearing gifts.* If you think something is too good to be true, you are probably right. Get away from it!
- *You must always be transparent.* Avoid playing into the hands of the personal agenda. Your only mission must be for the students. Make that crystal clear. Do not take secret meetings with individual board members. Information that you share with one must be shared with all.
- *There will always be some form of external forces on you. Understand that some local politicians will look to control you.*

Do You Have Five?

It sounds like we are playing some sort of game. We are not. We are talking about your career. We are talking about your qualifications and that promotion you seek. In many districts, it boils down to who you know rather than what you know.

I thought I had put my time in both as a curriculum supervisor and as a vice principal, and it was now time for me to be the principal. A principal announced his retirement from the smallest elementary school in the district, a perfect first principal job—or so I thought. I believed that I had all of the qualifications and experience, and more importantly, I thought that I had proven to be a real leader of people, both adults and students. I called the outgoing principal and asked if I could come over and talk about his school. We both knew each other as respected colleagues. He told me to come on over, but it really would not matter. I did not know or grasp what he meant.

I was still a bit bewildered by his response, but nonetheless still driven, and yes, still extremely naïve about the process. If I would have probed a bit more on the phone, we both might have saved some time. It was a quick meeting. We exchanged some pleasantries, and before I could ask my first question, he asked me if I had five. At that point in my career, I did not have a clue what he was talking about. He went into a bit more detail and asked me if I had my five votes for appointment secured on the board. We operated with a nine-member board, and for personnel appointments you always needed those five magical votes. I did not know if I had five votes. I never spoke to a board member. I never privately campaigned for the job. That was not my style. I saw his reaction, gathered my material, shook his hand, thanked him, and left. I did not get the job. I was never seriously considered. I did not have my five.

Leadership Lessons Learned

- *Know if you have your five.* Know who is really making the decision in your district. Then you can decide how and if you want to play those games. Sometimes, if you want to get ahead, you have to play those games.
- *You must learn to work a room.* Some people are masterful at this skill. These people may not be blessed with natural intelligence or leadership skill, but they are always in the know. Information is power. Relationships are power. Do not minimize this.

All in the Family

In many small towns, the school becomes the local employment agency. Husbands and wives, sons and daughters, uncles and aunts, and cousins of all sorts want to work together in a school. It may sound wonderful, but it puts an incredible stress on the operation of a building. This may seem especially odd coming from me because I was a product of this environment. I became an administrator in the district where my mother worked as a secretary. Believe me, this arrangement is not easy. On the surface, it may feel quaint and cozy, but the reality speaks differently. These arrangements are awkward and difficult to navigate.

Familial relationships on the job get in the way of conducting business. I also know that young educators sometimes meet their significant other at the workplace. If this was to occur, I would do my best to see that one of the teachers transferred from the building. You may be reticent because both are good teachers and you like both parties. This will be a painful breakup for you and the people involved. Nonetheless, one of them has to go. Please take my word for it. No matter what promises are made, eventually there will be an issue.

The same should be true if you decide to hire a child of a current teacher or staff member. You cannot support them working in the same building. Sorry, but this relationship will also get in the way. Run away from this. Run far away, and run very fast

I can also tell you that separating them by buildings may be fine for you as a building principal, but it might cause a negative ripple in the rest of the district. Often, it just doesn't work. I have been through this as both a principal and a superintendent. And if I had the opportunity to do it all over again, I would resist the temptation no matter how strong it may be.

Yet, the politics of the community or the school will pressure you and make it extremely difficult to stand by your beliefs on this matter. I encourage you to do your best to hold your ground on this one. However, if the local politics force you into this situation, make sure that your eyes are wide open. Set some ground rules that everyone can live by. And do not let this be the large elephant in the room that is never discussed. This must be spoken about honestly, with directness and candor. Remember that the aggravation and perhaps the career you save may be your own.

It is hard to live by this no-family rule, especially when you like the people and they are excellent teachers. They may care dearly about the school and children. On the other hand, they could be malcontents that probably do not like you, the students, or the district. I have seen it both ways. Your personal relationships will get in the way.

What will happen when you have a disagreement with one party? Will it spill over into your relations with the other party? You bet it will. What will happen if you feel the need to terminate one of the parties? Do you think that will impact your relationship with the other person? Of course it will. You know that. You did not get to where you are right now without possessing that little bit of common sense. When final evaluations are completed and one of the parties is unhappy, I can guarantee that the other person will not be happy. You see how this can snowball.

In any event, this myriad of family relationships within your school can be emotionally draining. Is it worth it?

Leadership Lessons Learned

- *Do you want family relationships in your building?* Sometimes it may be worth it and other times you will live to regret it. Think long and hard about it, because there will eventually be ups and downs in these relationships.
- *Understand that local community dynamics may directly work against you.* As a principal, you may just be told who you are getting. Do not moan. Do not groan. Coach the team that you are given.

Who Is Really in Charge? Not You!

You wake up one morning, the day after your board has appointed you to your principal's position, and you sit up in bed, when the revelation hits you that you are now the boss. Whoa! Not so fast. Do you really think so? I might have to differ with you. You may be the boss on paper, but who is really in charge? You soon will find out.

So, let's take a look at some potential lead characters who think they are in charge. Although I said think that they are in charge, they could very well be the person in command.

Let's play a new game. Will the real principal please stand?

The first one to his or her feet is your secretary. This person has been in this position for years and has seen many principals come and go. This is the all-powerful gatekeeper. Your secretary allows information and people into your world. He or she can control just about everything in your school life. This person is strongly opinionated and never hesitates to share his or her viewpoints. His or her desk is the seat of all rumors or gossip and most of the complaining in the school.

The next person to his feet is your head custodian. Just like your secretary, he or she has seen more than his or her share of principals come and go. This person walks around all day looking busy. He or she knows how to work the system and can be viewed as moody. If this person likes you, you are in good shape, but if not, watch out. He or she can be quick to point out a problem to you, but helping you solve it may depend on his or her mood. This person knows the job description well and knows other workers' job description just as well. He or she will readily share this knowledge with you. This person knows the power brokers in the community and also will share this with you. He or she also knows where all of the local skeletons are buried and is quick to point out to you the dirt that he or she has on someone.

The final contestant for the principal's job is your head football coach. You could substitute band director, theater coach, or favorite advanced placement teacher for the football coach. He or she finds his or her power in the relationships built over time in the community and the positive energy he or she has exhibited. This person is also perceived as a winner. Whomever this may be, as the principal, it is essential that you build a relationship with this person. At the end of the day, sometimes you will need this person. Do not forget this. I also must remind you that you may have several of these people. Now that becomes the real challenge. Juggling all of these strong personalities is a difficult and time-consuming job.

So what do you do? How will you deal with these principal pretenders? Each person will present unique challenges to you. And your list of imposters could go on and on. You must figure out how to work with each one of these people, or they will kill you off, piece by piece.

Leadership Lessons Learned

- *You can't go head-to-head in an all-out power war.* If you do, you will lose. You must build bridges and outmaneuver them.
- *These people are not going anywhere.* One of the sub-themes of this book is your ability to build and sustain relationships with a variety of people. Not all relationships are easy to build.
- *Learn what makes these people tick.* You may have to make small concessions to each person to keep moving forward.
- *Let the aforementioned people know that you are aware of their perceived power and appreciate them being on your team.*
- *Know that your decisions are your decisions. You have to believe in your decisions regardless of what these people think.* Your strength is in your ability to give away small pieces of your power to keep the machine moving. Working with these people will be time-consuming and energy sapping. However, I assure you that the more time you invest on the front end, the less time you will spend on the back end picking up pieces or trying to remove immovable obstacles.

Digging Deeper into the Issue of Politics

Leadership Lessons Learned

- *Some people are just insatiable!* You will quickly find out that some of the people within your community become impossible to please. You must not try to please them. Stop it right now!
- *You can get caught in a parallel universe.* You and your school may exist in one universe, and your outside political pressures exist in another universe. And they may never intersect. That is the sad part. The principal or superintendent must exist in both worlds. You cannot delegate this responsibility.
- *You must learn how to be the consummate politician. Never marginalize anyone!* Marginalization of an individual is perhaps one of the worst things that you can do to a person. This technique demoralizes and ultimately destroys the individual. Somehow you have to make the relationship work.
- *Know that you are always on the record.* The days of being off of the record are long over. Always assume that you are being recorded 24/7. Because of our smartphone technology, operate with the knowledge that your actions and words are always being recorded. Be careful!

Commandment 4
Thou Shalt Strive for Excellence, Yet Most People Are Very Happy with Mediocrity.

Complacency, the Poison of Excellence

Excellence is a destination. As educators, we are compelled to bring our students along on this journey—a journey that, if navigated successfully, will change lives.

All coaches start the year thinking they can win the Super Bowl or World Series. They can have that championship year. Although behind closed doors they can be realistic, no one starts the opening season speech imploring the team to win half of its games. It goes against the grain of what true leaders believe.

It is essential that your school's culture supports excellence. The pursuit of excellence can be seen within the culture of the school by observing a well-focused, engaged, and driven group of administrators, teachers, staff, students, and parents. All work is purposeful, and there is a drive to successfully accomplish both personal and school goals. There has to be a spirit of collaboration. There has to be a spirit of the team first. *You know a culture of excellence when you see it!*

Thriving in a culture of excellence requires thought, organization, and intense preparation. There are no shortcuts. The pursuit of excellence will be quickly derailed when one decides to take shortcuts

Complacency can kill excellence. When people become complacent, they do not perform up to their normal standards. They do not do as well as they are capable. If you can eliminate complacency from the culture of your school, performance and achievement will improve. People will also feel better about themselves. People may enjoy being there. They will intrinsically push themselves harder and ultimately produce better results. People may begin to hold each other accountable for the successful pursuit of excellence. You see this happen when a team starts to gel. Yes, your team (school) can gain momentum.

Mediocrity and complacency are like a cancer, and it must be sent into remission. If you do not address it, the cancer will spread and ultimately consume and kill any level of excellence. You can never settle, and you must always possess a relentless competitor's drive to succeed. *Your personal behavior matters, for you are the principal!*

Leadership Lessons Learned

- *Your culture must support excellence.* Do not neglect the culture of your school. You must consciously nurture it.
- *Complacency will sabotage your culture.*
- *You must always walk the walk.* People are watching you 24/7. They will model your behavior. Don't let yourself slip.

Don't Worry, Be Happy

Most people are happy being satisfactory. Most people are happy being mediocre. Most people are happy being just okay. If you disagree with me on this observation, wait until you have been a principal for a couple of years. For me, this has been one of the hardest lessons to learn. Some people just don't care about excellence. They don't care about winning that championship. They are just happy with a .500 record. They are happy cruising through life being okay. Why be okay when you can be excellent?

I find it more unbelievable when a school district will settle for being just okay. I have personally seen wasted potential in a community that was just happy being satisfactory. Excellence was not or never had been a goal. The students in this community could have achieved so much more if there was not this overriding feeling of maintaining the status quo. Parents would communicate to their children, "This school was okay for me, and it will be okay for you." There was never a need to push oneself. There was a feeling that resonated within the schools that it was not necessary to strive for greatness. One was never encouraged to upset the apple cart and think anywhere near outside of the box.

My meal last night was okay. My car is okay. The weather is okay. One could go on and on describing how we use this word. However, I did not want my school system, my administration, my teachers, my students, or my school being defined as being *okay*. This standard cannot be good enough for you. Excellence is not an easy path. It is much easier to be just okay.

Many years ago, I started seeing this pervasive complacency in my district. I started to call what I saw the contract of mediocrity. This is where the game of school is solidified (Fried, Waters). It is just like a binding contract, but there is never any paper signed. It is certainly covertly agreed to and lived by, but it always stays beneath the surface and is never talked about. It is time for you to talk about it.

The contract of mediocrity more or less binds the deal with a clear set of expectations that no one will push anyone. This starts with the student and includes all facets of the school community, including the administration, board, and parents. In these environments learning is not important; getting through the process unscarred is the critical piece. There is never any risk-taking or thinking outside of the box. There is this overriding feeling that you are not to push me, challenge me, or hurt me, and in turn, I will not disrupt you. In most schools, this is an institutionalized process. And if you do not play by the rules, you are either ostracized or pushed out.

Leadership Lessons Learned

- *Complacency can be pervasive in your school, if you allow it*
- *Push people.* People can drive themselves much harder than you ever expected. Do not allow people to settle because once you settle, it is so very easy to keep settling.
- *Do not allow people to get comfortable.* Once people get comfortable, it becomes easier to be complacent.

I Should Have! I Could Have!

Sometimes, you will just miss some things. You become blind to what is going on right in front of you. You could have a mess on your hands, and you do not even realize it is a mess. I experienced this type of situation in my first principalship. In retrospect, I doubt if I would have made the same mistake later in my career. You must always remember the theme of this book. Namely, you become a good principal by being a principal. There is no substitute for experience.

We had redesigned our middle school as a school within a school model organized around curricular themes. It was a dynamic place, with a vibrant young faculty, supported by a group of very wise senior teachers. The goal was to have the students with the same group of teachers for the three years they were in the school. This continuity of care was important to me. However, one of the "schools" had a higher rate of staff turnover, and new staff proved ineffective.

I tried to continually fill the staff with dynamic new teachers, and in each case, I struck out. Unfortunately, while the situation played itself out over the three years, I failed to adequately implement any catch-up plan for the students. Because of ineffective teachers, I think the students missed a lot. I should have moved some of my more-seasoned teachers into this program to help straighten it out. These teachers could have served as unofficial mentors and models for the new staff. They could have provided the leadership this program needed.

I should have added some enrichment opportunities for the students. I should have more closely monitored the implementation of the curriculum. I should have studied my data. I should have done more. I did not see the big picture. When these students went to high school, we had to, as a district, catch them up so they would be able to compete and be ready for college. Inasmuch as I moved with them to the high school, as their principal, I was able to closely monitor the situation. I think we were able to rectify any deficiencies that may have occurred in this process. I forgot about excellence and let mediocrity lead the way. I got caught in some of the bells and whistles of my programs instead of substance.

Leadership Lessons Learned

- *Data, data, and more data.* I did not use my data effectively to drive my decisions. Perhaps if I would have studied the data sooner, I could have averted this situation.
- *You must be forever mindful of the quality control of the curriculum.* What curriculum is being taught? What is really going on in the classrooms? It is your job to know!
- *Do not allow yourself to be tricked because everyone seems happy.* You must dig beneath the surface to find many answers. Happiness does not equate to effectiveness.
- *Know the big picture!* It is easy to get lost in the daily minutia.

Are You Going to the Beach? Are You Doing Some Yard Work? Are You Going to Teach?

What does your staff look like when they come to work? I believe one of the grossest examples of mediocrity is how poorly staff will dress to come to work. This communicates volumes about the person. I am also convinced that the students read the same message from teachers that I see.

I have seen teachers come to work in sundresses, dirty, collarless T-shirts, plastic flip-flops, and a whole assortment of clothes that I consider beachwear, loungewear, or clothes you use to mow the lawn, not to teach.

I also question whether some people have washing machines or mirrors. Perhaps they do but only see what they want to see.

I am also amazed at the teacher's strong affinity to wear blue jeans and denim to work. Although I certainly know that these jeans may cost hundreds of dollars, I question their appropriateness for teaching. To me, it suggests that you were outside doing some yard work, and you just decided to come in and teach for a minute. It sets the wrong image. As a child, I would put my dungarees on to go play. Many of you reading this book probably have never heard of that word. Yes, that is what our blue jeans were called many years ago.

Teachers would tirelessly work to circumvent this rule. I was amazed at some of the ideas that some would present to me to wear these jeans. Was it a power struggle? Were they really more comfortable? How a teacher looks and comports him or herself is extremely important. Teachers clamor to be treated like professionals, yet they will fight you to wear blue jeans and come to work slovenly. It does matter! I wish I could implement the requirement of wearing a tie at work. I am convinced the school's culture and climate would improve.

Leadership Lessons Learned

- *If you believe in a dress code, enforce it.* You respect what you inspect!
- *For some, self-pride is missing.* People just don't care. You may need to coach them. That is your job, the forever coach.
- *It* does *matter what your staff looks like!*

Digging Deeper into Excellence and Mediocrity

Leadership Lessons Learned

- *Sometimes you will be challenged to change things for the sake of change.* You may want to tinker with something that may seem innocuous. However, you will come to find out that your decision may have significant negative effects. I found this out when I contemplated lowering the standard for admission to the National Honor Society. When I thought about this in isolation, I thought it was a great idea. However, when I allowed more people into the decision-making process, I saw the deleterious impact my actions could have had. Be careful.

- *You must communicate your high expectations.* You must also provide a wide array of ways to attain those high expectations because no two people will travel the same path.
- *You must care what your stakeholders think and be aware of the implications for your decisions.*
- *Know the importance of the issue and your decisions.* Sometimes, you may think that the issue is not a big deal, and then all hell breaks loose.

Commandment 5

Thou Shalt Ensure Equity—Even though the System and People within the System May Work Against It.

Everyone Is Entitled to a Fair Shot

Frequently, you will be working against the system. This is especially true when you are trying to ensure equity for your students. The system can be stacked against you from the very beginning. It is your job to make sure everyone gets that fair chance. Even though your community may change, it is incumbent upon you to make sure there is a level playing field for your students regardless of their wealth or color.

It is easy to talk about equity, yet at times it is difficult to achieve. There may be hidden traps already in the system to make it difficult for a student of color or low economic status to get a fair chance.

Schools tend to be divided by color or wealth, and my school was no different. And in both of these cases, there is usually no one around to speak for these students. Biases are soundly entrenched within the system.

Many of your students are being forced to navigate this terrain by themselves. There is no one in the home who can speak for them. These are the students who are told what to do by a counselor or principal and are expected to quietly comply. The system is set up that way. It makes the adult's job in the school much easier. I do not know of any principal who relishes the argument with the knowledgeable and articulate parent. Principals will capitulate usually because they just do not want the hassle.

It is only natural. But who will speak for the underserved? It must be you. And at times, the first thing you must do is change the system.

I was amazed when I first heard of students having to navigate the entire college entry procedure by themselves. This is an incredible task. It is surprising how many students do this successfully. These young people have to figure out the SATs, the applications, and how the bills are going to be paid. Sadly, school guidance counselors tend to be nothing more than schedule changers and test administrators. That comment is not about them personally. The comment is a condemnation as to how schools have set up the role of counselor with its accompanying unmanageable student load.

You must make your decisions about what is right for the students, especially regarding equity, not what may be good for the adults. You may have to change the soundly entrenched status quo. *In the course of my decision-making, I have found that balancing the rights of the individual student versus the rights of the school community can be your most difficult test.*

In the course of your decision making, you may be harshly criticized. And there may be instances when you will be accused of making your decisions solely on race. Perhaps the most difficult thing to hear is when you are called a racist or bigot. The reverse can also be said of a decision you are making—namely that you are imposing some sort of your own brand of affirmative action. There are also times when someone may play the race card on you. I believe in my heart that few people actually believe this but nonetheless will use it to attempt to get what they may want. You must stay true to your vision. You must stay true to your belief that all students are entitled to the best education your school can provide.

You can also never make assumptions or have preconceived notions about race or wealth. For example, never assume that two people of the same race, gender, or wealth will have the same beliefs and needs. Each person is an individual. Never forget that.

Leadership Lessons Learned

- *The system can be set up to never ensure equity. It is your job to change it.*
- *You will be called upon to be the significant adult for many students.* Your students cannot navigate the path to life by themselves. If a parent or guardian is not present, the job falls to you. Do it.
- *You will always be challenged by the delicate balance between the rights of the individual and the needs of the school.* This will keep you up at night.
- *Lose your assumptions because they will only deter you and are most likely wrong.*

Damn It! Just Do the Right Thing!

This one was simple. This one should have been easy. But why was it allowed to happen in the first place? Why didn't somebody change it? I think you already know the answer.

When I first became principal of my school, it would not have taken a visitor too long to detect a huge inequity. If one was to have taken a tour of the honors and advanced placement classes, one would have seen classes that were made up of mostly white students. Some people may have found this surprising since the school was close to 70 percent African American and Hispanic at that time.

Something was wrong here, and for me it was so very obvious. Where were the African American and Hispanic students? No one seemed to care.

The problem was that there was an artificial bar placed on the entry into these classes. Students were being barred from these classes because of their previous year's standardized test score. It was just wrong! I jumped on this right away. Sometimes you cannot wait to build consensus, you cannot gather input, and you cannot overanalyze. You must act. And with a stroke of the pen, I did.

Believe me, I did try to build consensus among staff that this was the right thing to do, but I was amazed at the resistance I encountered. A large number of my staff was happy with the way it was. That in itself is a sad discourse on equity.

My solution, which seemed so simple, was to merely remove this test score requirement. *Changing course entry criteria was easy. Changing staff attitudes was hard.* For me, if students wanted to take these classes, they would be allowed to regardless of any criteria. The student was well coached that the teacher was not going to lower expectations or slow down. If the students were ready to accept the challenge, I welcomed him or her into these classes.

Over time, we did provide some tutorial services to help support students who accepted this challenge. In a few short years, if you took the same visit, I am proud to say that you would not have noticed any difference in the ethnicity of these classes as compared to other classes. I look back and upon reflection believe that this may have been my most important career accomplishment. It opened doors for students—all students. This seemingly small change allowed my African American and Hispanic students to successfully compete with the white students. I am very proud of that!

Leadership Lessons Learned

- *Always fight for equity.* Things are not always fair and equal. Your mission must be to provide equal opportunities for all students.
- *Be sensitive to the racial implications of your decisions.* You must know what needs to be done and then just do it.
- *Combat the racism of low student expectations.* This is perhaps one of the greatest disservices that we do to students. We do not believe they can succeed.
- *Use your data to uncover other areas that may suggest a less-than-equitable situation.* What about student suspension rates? Student special education classification rates? Attendance rates? My hunch is that these areas will be skewed against students of color.

It Is Survival of the Fittest, a Deadly Game

Many public schools are just waiting to die. Just like that stray antelope that gets picked off by the pack of lions, public schools are waiting to be picked off by that bright new shiny school of choice. It could be that public thematically driven selective magnet school or that well-established charter school. Soon it could be a voucher-driven parochial school. Your public school is marked.

I used to think that for my district, this was nothing more than white flight. As the district and community changed demographically, I saw this flight as nothing more than overt racism. It may have been subtle, but to me, it shouted racism. Families did not want their children to attend school with "those" kids. And for me, those kids meant our African American and Hispanic students.

One day, I had an epiphany as I noticed the migration of African American and Hispanic students out of the district. Maybe this white flight phenomenon had evolved into something a bit more complex. This was now really not about white flight. What I now saw was *bright flight.* Parents of all races wanted their children to be educated with children and families who have similar goals and values, regardless of race or ethnicity. For whatever reason, and for whatever misperceptions, people believed that my district was void of these students. The community had little faith that serious students existed in my school. Residents truly believed that the school was void of a commitment to achieve. Yet in reality, our students were able to pursue a full array of advanced placement courses; the school was safe; students went on to matriculate in top colleges and universities; and there was a range of cocurricular activities, most notably a nationally recognized performing arts department. Yet many parents and students looked to escape. I had to combat this bright flight or the school was doomed.

This phenomenon has been disguised and hidden for a variety of reasons. Some parents may argue for a parochial education guided by religious beliefs; some parents will argue for a private school environment because of the upwardly mobile status that they may enjoy; some parents will choose home schooling because the parent always knows best; and finally, some will abandon the public schools because some parents do not want their children attending school with "those kids." Today, "those kids" I define as the unmotivated, uncommitted, apathetic, lazy, or disruptive student. It did not matter what they looked like because they came in all sizes and colors. I believed that many residents viewed our school as the home for the disaffected. These are the youngsters who walk into school with an attitude that dares teachers to teach them. These are the students who drag down the class and have caused schools or teachers to lower their standards and water down their curriculum. Their parental commitment is weak not because of true apathy but an unfortunate lack of parenting skills and the realities of life. Many just did not have the time to provide academic leadership in the home. This all may sound like an excuse, but nonetheless, I believe it to be true. Bright students of all races were running out of the district. This was really driven home to me as I came to work one day and saw about fifteen students waiting on the corner for the bus to take them to a parochial school. The group represented the diversity of our community. There were white students, black students, and brown students whose families believed we could not effectively educate their children. I did not think for a minute that this was student choice. For most, that is a smokescreen. This was parental choice. Make no mistake about this. Parents want their child to be around children like them, and this far transcended the color of their skin. It was a new era. This new era was about achievement, not race.

One could argue that competition makes us all better. This is true when the playing fields are level. But for us to compete with these schools, we started at a marked disadvantage. First of all, as a public school, it was our task to educate all children. Second, we had to pass a school budget that was impacted by a tax levy that was capped. Our competitors did not have to do this. I do not believe choice the way it exists today operates with equity in mind.

Let's start with the entry process. The child needs a knowledgeable, committed adult to process the application and submit it in a timely and complete fashion. The parent has to be bureaucracy savvy to succeed. Choice continues to rob the public district of its potentially most important resource: its best and brightest students. Not only does the district lose a group of serious students, but the district also is unable to count them in test scores and achievement data. In a relatively small district, a handful of students may be the difference between making federal and state standards and receiving an acceptable or unacceptable rating. A school can get labeled as in need of improvement or failing because of one test score. It is almost impossible to overcome these school ratings. Negative ratings will cause more students to seek alternative choices. It becomes a vicious cycle.

So where is the answer? We can sit by and let our public schools die a not-so-slow, painful death, or we can be proactive and outsell and out-recruit the best of them. I was not going to be a spectator in this process. I had to act. I needed to fix instruction, personalize each school, fix the facilities, remove parent alienation, and actually provide meaningful teacher-directed professional development for the staff. I had to make sure we did the little things right.

Bright flight occurred because we allowed it to occur. We became complacent. We were the only game in town. This has changed.

We also allowed erroneous negative opinions to overtake those who believed positively about the school or district. I personally let misperceptions go unchallenged, and I did not clean up our own backyard.

Remember that If enough people speak loudly enough, even though they may be wrong, left unaddressed, it will suffocate any positive thinking. We were slow to embark on a positive marketing campaign. We failed to keep pace with how the new breed of schools packaged themselves and sold themselves to the parents and students. People will tend to fill a void in their thinking with whatever may be the loudest and most available message. Playing catch-up is hard.

Do not forget that bright flight can be an epidemic.

Leadership Lessons Learned

- *Your school must be competitive with other schools.*
- *You must make your school's message about achievement and excellence.*
- *Do a thorough analysis of your school and eliminate any inequity that exists.* Study your data. Does race play a role?

Where Are All of My Homies?

This was an interesting question posed to me by one of my brighter, more articulate students. At first I thought it was a very simple question, and I don't believe this young man intended this question to spark any deep reflection on my behalf. Yet it did. The question made me think deeply about my school, my vision, and my mission as the school leader.

It was the week before Christmas, and it was our school's practice to invite many of the recently graduated students who had entered college back to school to talk to the current seniors about the first semester of college. It was a nice event. It was both seasonal and warm. I am sure that most school districts do something like this. It is a real feel-good moment.

Over time, we started to only invite students to this event who were well on their way to college because our guidance department found over the years that too many students used this experience as an escape from class and were not really interested in hearing from the former students. At this point in time, my school was about 20 percent white, and the rest of the students were African American or Hispanic.

I was standing at the door, acting like a policeman (a principal's job many days), checking student entry passes. An African American student came to the door, and we started a brief conversation. I knew this student well and had a very good rapport with him.

As he entered the cafeteria, he froze in his tracks and exclaimed to me, "Where are all of my homies?" (Remember, homies at that time meant his friends or his peer group.)

I stepped back and looked. Something was wrong with this picture. Not one other African American male was represented in this group of invitees. I really could not believe my eyes. Something was wrong with the way we were doing things. Something had to change. As a school, we were missing something, and it was obvious by this picture. This catapulted me into a deep depression that caused some significant reflection. Personal reflection was fine, but action was needed.

Several days later, I called him into my office and shared how his statement impacted me. I probed as to why he was different. He talked about several things, the most important being the influence of his parents. He did not want to let them down. He also spoke about the positive influence of his teachers and coaches within the school. He went on to talk about how he felt that in ninth grade, he was at a crossroads and chose what he felt was the right path. It was a difficult choice, but he was both mature and intelligent. And he was able to stay strong in the face of his peer group. He also had the unique ability to flow in and out of his group without it being a problem. I have seen only several students have this uncanny ability to be accepted for who they were within their peer group and knowingly be able to change their demeanor and behavior based upon their surroundings.

You will not find it strange to hear that not only he but also his five brothers and sisters are all college graduates and are very successful. The young man I speak of currently is a successful businessman in the world of finance in New York City.

I think about why he and his siblings were successful graduates of my school and later college graduates. I can point to four factors, namely:

1. There were significant adults in his life, and they advocated for him. They also provided him a set of expectations that he felt were important.

2. He possessed a level of maturity that exemplified self-responsibility and a level of personal ownership and accountability regarding his life and future. He was also savvy about the game of school and knew how to successfully play the game. He had mastered the art of teacher-pleasing behaviors, while still maintaining his status among his peers.

3. He had a set of goals and expectations, perhaps set by his parents, but he was able to see the importance of these goals and was able to set a direction to achieve them.

4. For the most part, he was able to engage and focus on his objectives.

So, what did we learn from this, and what can we do about it?

Leadership Lessons Learned

- *We had to immediately evaluate everything that we did in our school to peel back the layers and see how we were reinforcing institutional racism in the way we managed things.*
- *We had to make sure that there were adults within the building to advocate for each student.* Although we could not be the parents of the students, we could certainly perform many of the roles of parents.
- *We had to work very early in the student's academic career to communicate high expectations and goal-setting activities.*
- *Students had to develop a sense of personal responsibility, and we had to guide them to get to this point.*

Digging Deeper into the Issue of Equity

Leadership Lessons Learned

- *Racists come in all colors.* Sometimes we think of racism with a solitary perspective. This is untrue inasmuch as racists come in every color. I would always share with a local advocate that his message got lost because of his racial overtones. He wanted to advocate for kids, but only African American students. Instead of listening, people tuned him out.

- *Some people will always yearn for the "good old days."* Some will find it hard to accept diversity. They do not want to hear Spanish being spoken in the hallways or on the soccer field. One faculty member wanted me to suspend a student for wearing her hijab in school. Others openly resented celebrating Black History Month and having any multicultural celebrations. For them, the good old days meant when the students were all white. *I am happy to report that thankfully these attitudes did not reflect the majority of the staff, yet their voices could be viewed as the vocal minority.* And of course, they would never speak this way in public. These people would slither into my office, shut the door, and in private express their opinions. I am very proud and honored to have worked with a group of teachers and staff members who chose to be in our school and respect and celebrate the diversity of our students.

- *Mine your data for equity.* You must study suspension rates, failure rates, and special education classification rates. I am willing to bet that they are skewed against the students of color. *Now do something about it!*

- *Hire the best teachers possible!* Yes, it is extremely important to hire teachers who look like your students. You must actively recruit candidates to fill your vacancies. *However, and I say this loudly, providing students of color with subpar teachers just because they may be black or brown is perhaps the most horrific example of racism that exists. I would not hire color over quality. All of our students need great teachers!*

- *When there is no advocate in the home, you must step up to help students navigate the educational process.* Make sure your staff knows this. Many students do not have the network at home to provide uniforms, costumes, shoes, or other requirements that the school may unintentionally place on the families. I have been blessed that my staff never let that peripheral stuff get in the way of a student participating and performing, A good coach or teacher can see this and work around it.

- *Do not judge!*
- *In addition to equity surrounding race, gender, or sexual orientation, schools can face a distinct prejudice against the poor or disengaged family.* The discrimination by wealth does not see color, religion, or orientation. It is all-encompassing.

Commandment 6
Thou Shalt Know That Thy Knowledge Is Thine Experience. Thy Graduate School Education Is Useless.

Useless, Useless, Useless!

Your graduate education is useless. I guarantee that when I put that statement in print, I will alienate all of my education professors. Sorry, but after a career in school administration, this has become my personal truth. My time and money could have been spent in a much better way. That is why I will argue that the way our profession trains both principals and teachers is obsolete. But that is not the purpose of this book. When you land your first principal position, do not delude yourself that you will be able to fall back on what you learned in graduate school. Also, do not waste your time digging through all of your coursework textbooks seeking answers. For the most part, these texts were written by professors who do not have a clue what actually happens in a school.

Leadership Lessons Learned

- *Your experience will guide you.* You become a good principal by being a principal. You must learn from your experiences. Find a mentor. Ask for advice. Ask for help. Build a network of supportive, critical friends.
- *You will be challenged daily with issues you never would have thought possible. Deal with them!*

Robbing One's Innocence, a Vile Crime, and a Despicable Man

I will not tiptoe around this topic because you see, in so many ways, I lived it. I had an up-close and personal view of a demon at work—perhaps the textbook definition of a pedophile. You will quickly see what I mean.

You would never learn any of this in a formal graduate school. I had a somewhat unique career path. I attended the school where I would someday be the principal. Several decades later, I would be the superintendent in the same district. I saw people and situations from several different perspectives. Many of the teachers I had as a student were still in the district when I became principal.

Like many of you reading this book, I probably became a teacher because of the influence of several teachers I had as a student. In many ways, I wanted to emulate them. Once again, this is not uncommon for young people when they are seeking their own self-identity. It is important that you understand this point to feel the impact of this story.

I was just moved from my principal's job (after thirteen years) and was settling into my new role of assistant superintendent when I started to receive some troubling emails claiming that the district had a pedophile on its payroll. These allegations were actually from a time when I was a student in the school and personally knew the victim.

These emails chronicled in detail long-standing sexual abuse by a teacher who was still employed in a part-time position in the district. I can only describe the allegations as horrible.

When I had an idea of where this was all headed, I picked up the phone and made two calls. The first call I made was to the state's child abuse agency, and the second call was to the local police department. If there is nothing else to learn from this book, understand that you are not the investigator in legal matters. This is serious stuff. Please do not mess it up, because if you do, the entire story will become about how you mishandled the situation rather than the facts of the real situation.

To make a long story short, through a myriad of meetings with the local police, prosecutors, and lawyers, it turns out that the offenses happened too long ago to prosecute and the perpetrator was protected by time. Yes, the statute of limitations had run out. There was nothing we could do except to fire the person from the extra service position. I had the good fortune of participating in that meeting. In the meeting, the person admitted to all the allegations leveled in the emails. When this admission took place, it was all I could do not to get up and kick his butt. I had to settle for verbally blasting him and yes, firing him. Yes, my response might be considered immature, but it was visceral. He was nothing but a contemptuous fraud and a criminal. He was escorted out of the building, never to been seen again. Not long after this event, he quietly passed away. What he did was unforgivable. My gut tells me that this could not have been an isolated case.

I always thought of myself as a mature individual, and I was clearly in the last quarter of my career, but on this day when I confronted him, I grew up a bit more. He was one of my heroes growing up, and now he was destroyed. He was one of the people I most wanted to be like. I probably became a teacher in part because of his influence. This myth of a man now sat in the office as a real coward: a violator of children, a thief of their innocence, and a destroyer of lives. He violated almost everything I believed in about teachers.

I am glad that he is dead and hope his victims were able to get some relief and closure upon his passing.

He was never talked about in the district again as long as I was there. I believe that some of the old timers really knew and just kept silent for all of those years. And if that was the case, shame on them. I hope they cannot put their head on the pillow at night without thinking about this. The community never knew, and there were times I had to stop a community group's plans to honor this individual. He knew how to manipulate. He knew how to deceive. He knew how to build trust. He knew how to ruin lives!

Leadership Lessons Learned

- *Where there is smoke, there is usually fire.* If you think that something is wrong, it probably is. *Do something about it!* Call the authorities at once. Do not think you can handle it. As this was happening years ago, I strongly believe that people knew about it yet did nothing about it. Perhaps they did not know what to do. And yes, perhaps it was just easier to put your head in the sand.
- *Keep good records, and always document everything.* You need accurate and precise notes. Now is not the time to cut corners or be sloppy.
- *Never let personal relationships cloud your decision making.* If you allow this to happen, you may be guilty of allowing the wolf to play among the lambs. Remember that pedophiles are master manipulators. Negligence includes seeing or knowing something and doing nothing about it.

Has It Gone This Far? You Bet It Has.

When I think back to the start of my administrative career, I would have never dreamed of having to deal with guns in my school. But as times changed, so did my mindset. On top of all the other responsibilities that came with being a principal, I now had to think about guns. That was a new reality. And yes, as times continued to change, I had to deal with more types of emergency drills than I could have ever imagined. Where did the days go when a principal only had to worry about doing a couple of simple fire drills every month? Times had changed right before my eyes.

I was out in the building when I was called back to my office, where a student was claiming that she had seen a handgun in a student's backpack. I was a bit skeptical. I still thought that the notion that one of my students would bring a gun to school was crazy.

I took her seriously, sent her back to class, picked up one of my teachers (I would never do this alone), and we went and got the young man from his class, making sure that he had the book bag with him. Never go alone. I surprised him by my visit. I asked the student to accompany me to the office for a brief discussion. *(Always remember, when you are seeking a student for a significant issue, have an adult go get them, and never let them out of your sight. Never send for a student who is emotionally upset and perhaps indicating thoughts of suicide to report to your office unattended. Students in crisis need adult supervision and can never be left on their own, even to report to an office.)*

A recurring theme in these case studies is that students will be your biggest source of information. Take them seriously. Cultivate your resources. Cultivate your relationships. Students tend to tell you the truth, and the more they trust you, the more information you will be able to gather.

When I got to his class, nothing seemed out of the ordinary, but I did notice that he had left the backpack on his desk. I personally retrieved it, and when we arrived in the office, I asked him if it was all right to search his backpack. (As a school administrator in my state, I only needed a reasonable suspicion to make this search, unlike a police officer, who would have needed a probable cause.) I always had someone with me to observe the procedure. As soon as I opened the backpack, I saw a large silver-plated handgun. My confiscation of the gun was smooth and incident free. I maintained personal possession of the firearm and called the police, who responded and escorted the young man to the station in handcuffs. *This happened years ago. I know today you have specific procedures developed in conjunction with your local police. Follow their directives.*

Prior to his exit, though, he shared more information about the reason why he carried the gun, and he claimed it was for protection. I never learned who he needed protection from and I doubt if that was true, yet nonetheless, he felt a need to carry the gun. The ironic part for me was that he had hidden the bullets in the courtyard right outside of my window.

We held an expulsion hearing in accordance with our district policy and law. Eventually the young man was placed in an alternative school to finish his schooling and was removed from the district. Unbelievably, at the hearing, a board of education member asked me if the student may have felt that he needed the weapon and that perhaps I was overreacting. He wanted me to give him another chance. I had a hard time maintaining my composure at the lunacy of that remark. I stood my ground. Bringing a weapon to school crossed my personal line in the sand. He could not stay.

Unfortunately, the student's lifestyle never changed and only worsened. Several years later, he was killed in a high-speed car chase on a local highway—a life truly wasted.

I had to deal with guns twice more in my career. Thankfully, I was successful, and no one got hurt. One young man was carrying the weapon in his coat pocket. He was wearing the coat inside out. Just think of it— an inside-out jacket gave you two built-in pocket holsters! From that day forward, when I saw someone wearing a coat or sweatshirt in this manner, I became suspicious and checked it out. The last gun I retrieved was when a young man had hidden a weapon on school grounds. When I was alerted to this, I found his hiding place fairly easily. In each case, I was able to remove a weapon from the school because of a tip a student brought me.

Weapons of All Sorts

Over my career, I have confiscated knives, brass knuckles, and an assortment of handmade items that could be used as a weapon. I can vividly recall a situation that played itself out in the newspaper. One of my students made a small bat or what I would refer to as a billy club at the shared time vocational school. He carried this item in his bookbag, with the top five inches sticking out of the top, with a taped handle grip, and another student told me that he referred to this as his n----- beater. He later affirmed this to me. You should also know that this student was an African American young man.

I suspended the student, recommended expulsion, and brought criminal charges against him. To me it was clear that he knew exactly what he was doing. I was painted as the villain in the newspapers, but I stood strong. I took a beating in the press, but to me it was worth it. I believed I was doing the right thing for all of the people in my building. I believe that my staff and most of the parents thought I was doing the right thing.

I feel compelled to put a disclaimer in the book here and tell you that despite the stories that I shared about weapons, please remember that this was over almost a thirty-five-year administrative career. I strongly believe that for an urban school with at times upward of sixteen hundred students enrolled, we did pretty well. No one ever got hurt as a result of any sort of weapon.

Leadership Lessons Learned

- *Your relationship with students will give you access to a great deal of information.* Students want to feel and be safe.
- *Understand that your school reflects society.* Whatever is going on outside of your walls will find its way into your school. You must prepare for every potential situation.
- *Know where your line in the sand is, and make sure the entire school community knows this.* For me, if you brought a weapon, sold drugs, or put your hands on a teacher in anger, you had to go. There were no second chances. *You must be consistent.*
- *Student safety must always be your primary concern and focus.* If the students and the staff feel unsafe, no learning can happen. Put all of your other initiatives on hold until you feel that your school is safe and orderly. I know for some new principals, this could take several years. It is always about school culture.
- *Know that sometimes you will get beaten up by the press.* Stand for what you believe in, and let others say what they may. Additionally, stay away from any social media forum, for in all likelihood you will at times get beaten up. You or your family do not need to see this.

Good Morning, Vietnam; Farewell, My Friend

Over the course of your career, you will work with thousands of students. Every now and then you encounter that very special student—the one that has it all. He or she is smart, personable, mature, and talented and already knows how to work that room. He or she possesses unlimited potential. Your former students will accomplish remarkable things. And when they do, you sit back with pride and only hope that you in some way were part of this success. There are other times when your former students will just break your heart. These are the things no one ever teaches you. No one ever talks about these situations. You are on your own. These are the situations that will trouble you the rest of your life.

The president of the student body is missing. He hasn't returned home, and no one knows his whereabouts. He handled the morning public address announcements every day. Everyone noticed his absences. He was entertaining and enthusiastic. He would mimic Robin Williams, greeting the student body in a similar fashion as Williams did in the movie *Good Morning, Vietnam* (1985). I believe this young man idolized Williams and how he played the role of Adrian Cronauer in the movie. Cronauer wanted to shake up Vietnam. This young man wanted to shake up our school. He was involved in every activity in school, and both teachers and fellow students loved him. He had such a bright future. Yet he was a troubled soul.

He was absent from school and missing from his home. After several days, I decided to make a home visit. I spoke with his father, who was terribly worried about his son. The young man was an Asian American adopted by this American family at a very young age. The father was confined to a wheelchair and did gun repair from the home to make a living. He asked me to please go into the garage and check to see if the young man was there.

Just imagine the dread that I felt in the few minutes it took me to walk into the garage and open the door. I expected to see the worst, namely the young man dead in the garage. It seemed like an eternity for the garage door to open. Luckily, the garage was empty.

Several days later, I was seated at my desk when I picked up the phone, and on the other end was a representative from Covenant House in Anchorage, Alaska. My missing student was there. It was one long trek from New Jersey to Alaska, and no flying was involved. We learned later the student was trying to get to Vietnam, his birthplace.

He was returned to our school community by Covenant House and resumed his normal activities. Yes, he was in counseling, and we made sure he had what we thought were the proper supports in his classes and overall in the school day.

Several weeks later, my phone rang again. This time, I sadly learned the very worst news that I thought possible. The young man had committed suicide by taking a gun from his father's work area and shot himself.

I was devastated. The school was devastated. His suicide rocked the community. We had to mourn his loss and yet make sure the school survived. How could we do both? And this was way before the time of any formal suicide prevention or postvention training was required by schools.

In one small way, our school was progressive. We had just started a crisis team and had done some informal work preparing the school for a multitude of potential tragedies. We did all right. There was no contagion effect, and although we were never the same, we soon returned to the business of teaching and learning. You can pick up one of the hundreds of books now written on this topic and find out that we did most of the things suggested to recover from this loss. We were complimented by outside agencies on the way in which the school handled his death. I will never forget this young man. Many staff members and students were deeply affected by this trauma.

We learned a great deal about ourselves and our school community in dealing with this tragedy. In retrospect, I find it so ironic that both this young man and his idol, Robin Williams, died by their own hand.

I still hear his voice coming over the public-address system in the school, and I can close my eyes and see his effervescent face running down the hallways. Some things you never forget.

Leadership Lessons Learned

- *In times of crisis, your school will need to see and feel your strong leadership.* You have to show maturity, emotional strength, knowledge, and probably most importantly, confidence. At the end of the day, you will be judged for how you do in these highly stressful times. You must be a positive presence.
- *Let your people who are trained and have specific tasks in crises do their jobs.* Now is not the time to micromanage. You have to be the orchestra leader keeping all the instruments playing together. It is a hard job.
- *You and your school must continue to evolve.* You must be progressive and learn to do new things. We were successful in part because we had formed the crisis team in the building and started to learn about these issues and train for them. Nobody told me to start this team. I had the foresight to get the ball rolling.
- *Take good notes.* After the school returns to a degree of normalcy, debrief with your team. Be critical of your efforts and accomplishments. Know where your team excelled, and know where change must occur. This must remain a dynamic process.

Whack, There It Is!

I was never that naïve to think that fights would not happen in my school. As long as schools have been around, young people have resorted to violence to solve problems. I get that. Seeing a periodic fight in a school was to be expected. Yet, if it was to be expected, why was it never talked about in principal's school? I was never mentally prepared for what I was about to see.

I would try to spend my time in the students' cafeteria. Any time you place three hundred students in closely confined quarters, anything is bound to happen. An adult presence that is proactive can prevent many problems. An adult presence who just sits on the windowsill or chats with a colleague, oblivious to the environment, is useless. Make sure your teachers know what is expected of them during cafeteria duty. For a more important reason, being in the cafeteria gave me a good opportunity to get to know the students on a more personal level. Students can also see you in a bit of an informal manner. A smoothly run lunchtime will help ensure a smoothly run day. Do not underestimate this!

As I was standing in the cafeteria, a young man walked casually up to a young lady approximately ten feet from where I was standing and entered into a conversation with her. I was looking right at them. Everything seemed fine. Within a moment, seemingly without provocation, he reached back and punched this young lady as hard as he could squarely in the face.

I watched in horror and helplessness. No one could have reacted quickly enough to prevent this horrible act. Although I was looking directly at the pair of students chatting, I never saw it coming. To this day, I can hear the sound of his fist hitting her face. It was a one-punch event. It reminded me of the first *Rocky* movie where Sylvester Stallone is hitting the frozen side of beef as a training exercise. The sound was both awful and memorable. I quickly removed the offender from the area, and a colleague was able to escort the young lady to the school nurse. Thankfully, she only received bruises and some minor cuts. No bones were broken. I still do not know how that was possible.

Although I have seen students fight before, I have never heard a sound such as this. It was indescribable. Fist to face and bone to bone. My senses were also offended because it was a boy hitting a girl. This was unheard of when I grew up. It both horrified and offended me. We dealt with the young man as a school and with the police. The reason for this atrocious act turned out to be nothing more than some adolescent boy-and-girl nonsense. However, it was a rude awakening for me inasmuch as I had never seen a boy strike a girl. Sadly, it wouldn't be the last time I saw this. This episode occurred very early in my administrative career. I grew up some that day. I had my eyes opened that day. It changed me. Boys hit girls, and girls hit boys. Times change and not always for the better.

Leadership Lessons Learned

- *Manage your school cafeteria.* Make sure surveillance cameras are in the cafeteria. Also, never forget that each student now has a cell phone and is recording all the action. Be on your best behavior!
- *Make sure your staff is doing their job in the cafeteria.* Make sure they know your expectations and hold them accountable.
- *The rules of the game continue to change.* You must change with them.

Digging Deeper into Your Knowledge And Experience

Leadership Lessons Learned

- I can recall being called by a neighboring police department and asked if I could come and identify the decaying body of one of my teachers who had been out of school on a medical leave. As I was making my way to the car, my secretary ran out and told me that my services were no longer needed. *How did this person become so anonymous that no one missed her? How come we did not check in more with her?* Somehow, we just became too busy. Out of sight, out of mind! Shame on us!
- *If you stay in the job long enough, you will have to deal with death.* You have to be prepared to go to a family's house perhaps on a weekend to express your sympathy and do some informal counseling with a family who just lost a child. Always bring someone with you. Develop a checklist of activities for such an event. This will help ensure that you do not forget a critical piece of information that needs to be shared.

- *You must build relationships throughout the entire community, not just within your schools.* You must know your families, know your churches, know your pastors, and know your available community resources to call on. Do not be afraid to seek these individuals out. Communities tend to rally in times of crisis.
- *Don't forget to take care of your staff. Don't forget to take care of yourself. You can't go down in times of crisis.*

Commandment 7
Thou Shalt Lead with People and Collaboration. Always Understand That Thy Job Is All about Relationships.

Can You Manage the Sandbox?

Perhaps I am just not a quick learner because it took me years to figure out that you need people and that a *principal's job is all about relationships.* Do not make my mistake. Know that simple fact going into your first job. I always thought I was fairly intelligent and could out-work everyone. Believe me, it doesn't operate that way. You cannot set yourself up as an island. You cannot be that lone wolf and expect to be successful. The lead sled dog needs a team.

Good principals empower people. A good principal makes sure that the people around him or her are vested in the operation of the school. A good principal gives credit and praise to others. A good principal shows gratitude. It has to be more than a job for them. It has to be a passion and a personal commitment. With empowerment comes responsibility. When each person feels as though they share in the decision making, it becomes easier for them to feel a sense of responsibility in the production of the end products.

Collaboration is a nice buzzword. However, collaboration cannot just be a concept that is talked about. Collaboration has to be lived on a daily basis. Everyone is working together with their oars in the water, all pulling in the same direction. You will be able to see it and feel it. Collaboration has to be a foundational element in the culture of your school.

That leads me to the title of this segment: *Can you manage your sandbox?*

Just think about the people and the relationships that you must somehow juggle on any given day. You have teachers, paraprofessionals, secretaries, custodians, other administrators, your superintendent, your parents, your board of education, and your community at large. Let's never forget our coaches and extracurricular advisors because they can really eat your time and emotional resources. And each one of these people has a different frame of reference and maybe a different agenda. Most people are interested in only what is good for them. And with all of these people in your sandbox, how long will it take for a conflict to arise? Probably instantaneously.

Things may move along nicely for a while, but sooner or later, the bully will appear. The principal may inevitably have to come in and restore peace and order to the sandbox, but every time that happens, it eats away at the culture of your school.

Know that you will never win if you have disruption in the sandbox. And you can never ignore problems because they will not just go away. Left unaddressed, problems will only fester and in all likelihood bring more people into the problem.

Nonsensical drama seems to thrive in schools. You will never eliminate it, yet you must minimize it. You must also be very aware of how one person can disrupt the chemistry in your sandbox. If you do not believe me, just go to a playground and watch the children play. What happens when a child that doesn't play well with others enters the sandbox? An entire new group somehow forms with new norms and practices. The same will happen in your school.

Leadership Lessons Learned

- *Relationships, relationships, relationships.* Never forget that your job is all about people.
- *Empower people.* Develop a shared decision-making model.

- *Show gratitude.* Praise and reward your staff. You must stay in the background.
- *The chemistry of your teams continues to evolve.* Are you prepared for the drama and the arrival of the bully?

"I Like Children If They Are Properly Cooked." W. C. Fields.

Nice title. Nice quote to be used in a movie (*Tillie and Gus*, 1933), but how appropriate is it when one discusses a school?

I always took it for granted that those who pursued a career in education loved children. It was always a stock answer in most interviews. The candidate would always tout how much he or she enjoyed being around youngsters. Of course, some lied. For those candidates that were not truthful with me, we tried to weed them out. Sadly, some make a career out of disliking children. Why these people chose education as a career is well beyond my comprehension.

Some people chose this field just to be able to boss around someone for the entire day. It was a distorted sense of power. Others chose this field as a matter of convenience

I was fortunate in many ways that my school was around a metropolitan area and was a rich environment for pharmaceutical companies. I can vividly recall a time when the industry was going through a downsizing and there were a great many scientists looking for work. I interviewed some real geniuses. Some of these people had written books, held numerous patents, and now thought they could teach. I met a lot of brilliant people and had some stimulating conversations but found very few, if any, teachers.

I found it quite humorous as most of these scientists thought teaching was a breeze. It would be no big deal, and they thought they could do it with one hand tied behind their back. They would teach a few years and coast into retirement. For those I gave a chance to teach, they quickly learned how difficult teaching is. Few were successful.

One day, I was interviewing a gentleman for a chemistry teaching job, and I thought I had hit a homerun. Almost as an afterthought, I just happened to ask the candidate if he liked children. The silence was deafening. He stroked his nonexistent beard and said, "I am not sure." I almost fell off of my chair.

I needed to fill this position because I had my best and brightest students in need of a teacher. The board and parents were starting to breathe down my neck. Let's face it: I was panicking. Should I hire this man who had many of the things I was looking for, or should I keep on looking? It did not take me long to know what to do. After this reflective pause that seemed like an hour, I decided to pass on him. I very nicely explained to him that for me the interview was now over. I could not bring someone on board who was not sure if he or she liked children. No matter what intellectual capacity he could bring to the school, the first thing you must be able to do is to build those relationships with the students. I was not convinced at all that he could do this. He loved his science. I am not sure if he would love the kids. The candidate and I shook hands, and I think he appreciated my candor. I do not know if he ever went on another teaching interview.

Leadership Lessons Learned

- *Anyone hired in your school must like children.* Children are our clients. They are who we work for. Let us never forget this.
- *No matter what the external pressure might be, do not hire someone just for the sake of hiring someone.* If you do, you will regret it.
- *You might be able to help someone learn the pedagogical skills or the content, but you will never be able to help them like children.*

Hey, the Kid Was Right! You Are What You Are.

Let's face it—sometimes the kids are just right. They will see and say things that we perhaps do not see or perhaps we see, yet are reluctant to comment about. I regret that I did not keep a log of all of the great things my students said. Much of what was said was accurate and were things that I believed were true. My position prevented me from perhaps saying the exact same things. I think you will see how the following scenario exemplifies this and how my response was not the best of responses. I could have done better.

Over time, I have learned the importance of school culture and climate. My personal evolution has now been completed, and I believe that just about everything that happens in your school will refer back to the culture and climate established in your school. When something good happens, the culture helped allow it to happen, and when something bad happens, the same can be true.

This story clearly reflects a negative school culture. It reflects a student versus teacher culture, and it reflects on a power trip by a specific adult. Most of my students arrived for school through several front doors in the building. Most students walked to my school, and for some it was quite a distance. As the bell was sounding, students were running and hustling into school to avoid being late. A teacher was manning one of the doors, and as a student was about to hit the sidewalk to enter, he slammed the door in his face and told him he was late and now he had to go to the late entry portal and receive his disciplinary consequence for being late. Let's remember that some of my students walked two miles to school in all sorts of weather, were also working part-time jobs, taking care of siblings, and were doing a great many things that should have been reserved for adults. Upon seeing the teacher's action, the student flipped out and called the teacher an asshole. I was down the hall and heard the exchange. Of course, the teacher quickly wrote the student up on a disciplinary form and could not wait to submit it to me.

I am not proud to say that I blew this one. It was early in my career, and I blindly supported the teacher and suspended the student for disrespect. I wish I could get a do-over on this one.

I clearly let the student down. I wish I could have suspended the teacher. I wish I could have fired him on the spot. No wonder there was a lack of trust between students and teachers when they had to encounter this type of behavior. And I just piled on. Any hope of me establishing trust with this student just flew out the window. Of course, the student should not have said this. I am not condoning it. But I might have said the exact same thing. No wonder our school culture was not good.

I wish the teacher would have facilitated hustling the student to class and maybe gave him a little pat on the back for trying to get there on time. It has been many years since this incident occurred, but I want to, in absentia, offer my apologies to that student. He expected better of me, and I should have delivered.

Leadership Lessons Learned

- *Everyone in the school is responsible for the development of the school's culture and climate.* For years, I was shamed into thinking that this was just the principal's job.
- *With an effective leader (principal), people will know how to communicate and respect one another.*

No Room at the Inn

Sometimes there is just no room for you. You do not fit. You are the square peg in a round hole. It took me a while to understand that when you become an administrator, on a personal level, things change. I never wanted to believe this. I thought we all could be above these childish games. But I was wrong.

One of my former superintendents once shared with me some of his wisdom. He told me very succinctly that you have no friends. I was upset and surprised by his observation. Once again, it took me while to understand this concept.

You will have to make your own mind up about this observation. However, I do caution you about this. It is hard to be over at someone's house on a Friday night or seated at the same lunch table daily and then have to correct or discipline that same person on Monday. Or perhaps try saying no to this group. I tried it. It didn't work for me.

You think you were one of the lucky ones. Namely, you were promoted from within the district to your role as a principal. You are about to begin your transition. Your first day starts with an excitement and a sense of exhilaration. Your morning flies by, and it is now lunchtime. You have a break in the action, so you head over to the faculty dining room. You grab your food and sit with the same group of guys you have sat with for years. The minute you sit down, you notice that something is different.

I admit that at times I am a bit thick headed, and it took me a few minutes to realize what was happening. I was trying to figure out what had changed. What was wrong? What was different? The only thing that had changed was a title after my name. I was no longer welcome by my group who I thought of as professional friends. Although I was the same person, the title now made me quite different.

Sadly, this was the culture in my school. It was an us-and-them mentality. The us was the teachers and the them was the administration. My appointment as a principal made everything different. I was no longer welcome. I persisted for a few days, never really addressing the elephant in the room, and then stopped going into the dining room. I ate by myself at my desk. I was no longer one of the guys. I retreated to the isolation felt by so many principals.

As I matured and our culture started to improve, I gradually worked my way back into the dining room. Once there, I made a conscious decision to sit at a different table and with a different group of people every time I was there. My presence had an interesting effect on people. For some, I could tell that me being at their table caused some personal jitters. They now became uncomfortable, not me. This feeling did change over time. A more welcoming and collegial environment started to develop. It was now not an oddity to have a principal sit with the teachers at lunch. I thought we started to have a more normal adult relationship. We could interact over this small half hour of time without our roles or positions mattering.

There were other times when I would be invited to after-school or event get-togethers with the staff. I am sure the person who invited me probably was the recipient of some dirty looks or nasty conversation behind his or her back. Nevertheless, I would try to attend. I thought it was always positive that if invited, I should show up.

People would break into little groups for conversation and reverie, and I would be left standing by myself. When my wife was included, we would end up having a conversation with each other. It was quite obvious when we tried to enter a group for discussion that the conversation would either stop or quickly be redirected. I felt unwelcome by most people at these events.

To really see culture and climate change, you need to work hard to eliminate the us and the them. There has to be one team working together to make the school and the students successful. As long as the two teams exist, I just do not think that you will get to that promised land of a highly functioning school.

Leadership Lessons Learned

- *Relationships change.* Get used to it
- *You may have to work through and around unfair stereotyping.* The two-team paradigm will be hard to break.
- *You are not your job, although some people will never see that.* Some people may be jealous. Some people may be resentful, and others will feel a need to be angry just for the sake of being angry at a boss.
- *It is also crucial that you always maintain a bit of an army that will have your back and stand with you when the trail gets rough to navigate.* If you trample on people, they will never stay in your army. Every principal needs this army. I am asking you to be genuine and real with people. Never forget that you need people!

Learning from Dysfunction

If there is any lesson to be learned from this book, it is to check your emotions at the door. Grow some thick skin, and develop the ability to let things merely roll off of your back. You must become immune to the hurtful things that will be said about you or your decisions.

To set the stage effectively, I think it is important that you know that I am a former coach who can be loud and demonstrative. I have consciously worked on my softer side and have come a long way in this regard. I can also be quite physically intimidating, standing at six-foot-three and weighing in at 275 pounds. I am not easily pushed around physically or emotionally. I can hold my own with most people. However, there once was one particular student and father who knew how to push my buttons.

Over the course of the year, the father and I skillfully employed the art of brinkmanship until one day it all blew up.

Both the student and the father were perhaps the most difficult parent/child team I ever had to deal with in my career. Both the father and the son were emotionally challenged.

I was the middle school principal, and this young man was in constant trouble. No one could refocus him or control him. His father and I were at constant odds because I could not keep the child in school the way he behaved. Likewise, the father did not want him at home because I think it became a potentially lethal battleground between the father and the son.

The delicate balance of our relationship came to a head one day when I was sending him home again for disrupting the school. Please understand that when he disrupted, he disrupted everyone!

The father stormed into my office. The discussion quickly escalated. We soon found ourselves standing nose to nose with each other, waiting to see who would throw the first punch. He claimed that his son misbehaved because he could not read. I claimed we could not teach him to read because he could not behave. The old chicken-or-the-egg game. I could not take him or his son anymore, and he could not take me or the school anymore. Somebody had to give.

To this day, I do not recall how the situation deescalated, but it did. Although it seemed like an eternity, after a few seconds, we both backed off. We both lowered our voices, and the tension in the room abated. Luckily, the student was not in the room.

I knew better. I should have never let myself get into the situation. But sometimes your emotions can take over. We eventually were able to place the young man into an appropriate out-of-district school more suited to deal with his disability. I never learned if he ever learned to read, but I know he never learned to behave.

There were many times that the young man could engage in some insightful conversations. He told me one day that if someone ever entered his telephone booth, he would knock him or her out. I totally believed him and got it.

For anyone with a space problem, it can be a powerful illustration. I shared this lesson with many people. When people thought in terms of the telephone booth, they seemed to comprehend the idea of personal space.

Today, the only problem with this example is to go find a telephone booth. However, there is another lesson to learn here for the adults in your school. They need to respect the student's space and more importantly, keep their hands off of them.

Leadership Lessons Learned

- *Control your emotions.* There is no excuse for losing your control
- *Never meet with anyone alone.* Have a fellow administrator or teacher in the room to serve as a witness to this type of meeting. This third party could also have a calming influence in the room.
- *Let words roll right off of your back.* I let them get under my skin.
- *Who was right, the father or me? More importantly, did it matter?*

- *Coach your staff to keep their hands off of students.* If you feel the need to direct, coax, or move a child, put your hands in your pockets.
- *Respect everyone's space.* Stay out of people's telephone booth.
- *Deal with the mental health of your students.*

Digging Deeper into Collaboration and Relationships

Leadership Lessons Learned

- *You will spend a great deal of time dealing with adult to adult conflict.* I also believe that the healthier your culture is, the less you may have to deal with this. Often this conflict will involve your support staff, people such as your custodians, secretaries, paraprofessionals, and bus drivers. These employees will tend to just eat your time with pettiness.
- *Some people just can't get along with people.*
- *Intervene early in mediating staff conflict. Problems will not resolve themselves.* Never be surprised when people start throwing things or become physical. Some people only know how to settle their differences with violence. They do not possess the personal skills to handle it differently. You may have to teach them. You also may have to get rid of them!
- *All negative and toxic relationships detract from our mission of educating the children.*
- *Some people just enjoy playing mind games. They love drama.*
- *Your adults must keep their hands of off the children.* There are very few times that one needs to physically intervene. And for me, this includes hugs. Why do people feel so compelled to hug? I have seen these hugs lead to big trouble. And I recognize that any early childhood educator will argue with me on this topic. Okay, I get it. That kindergarten student may need that daily hug. But does that senior in high school?

Commandment 8
Thou Shalt Know Thyself. Always Communicate What Is Important to Thee.

I Am Who I Am!

You have to be about something. You have to stand for something. Being true to yourself is a good starting point for your leadership journey.

You need to be comfortable in your own skin. I like to think I was my own person, and I like to think that I set a standard for my staff and my students. My standard was excellence.

For me it started with *Ed's Four Es for Excellence.* My framework guided me on my leadership journey. If there is nothing else that you get out of this book, please remember my Four Es. They are:

- *Expectations*: You must start by holding high expectations for yourself, your staff, and your students. You must believe that you can win every game. And if you are not sincere about this, people will see right through you and you will become a fraud. *You can never be satisfied.*
- *Enthusiasm:* Every day you must bring a high level of enthusiasm to the job. I am convinced that your high energy is contagious. If you are excited, those around you will be excited.
- *Empowerment*: When you give people a voice, their level of commitment will rise. They will be more apt to accept

responsibility and be accountable. They will have pride in their work and accomplishments.

- *Environment*: It is your responsibility to create the environment that supports excellence in your classroom, school, or office. Everyone must know that when they enter your area, it is a place of excellence. Students see the inconsistencies that may abound in your school. I can go into a classroom with a given set of students and see a stellar learning environment—a classroom where students are engaged and committed. Then I can walk next door to the adjacent classroom a period later with the exact same students and see chaos. The only variable is the teacher. One teacher gets it, and the other teacher doesn't. Students will respond to whatever their expectations are.

Leadership Lessons Learned

- *Be true to yourself.* Stand for something.
- *Never forget the four Es: enthusiasm, expectations, empowerment, and environment.* Pay attention to the details!

Do You Know Who You Are? Do People around You Know Who You Are?

These are two very interesting and important questions. Do you know what is really important to you? And how do you communicate this?

Everything starts with your vision. You are who you are because of your vision. You lead the way you lead because of your vision. You will make decisions based upon your vision. It is that important. For those reading this book who cannot articulate their vision, it is essential that you stop now and begin to hone your thoughts. What do you believe in? What do you hold sacred? Before others can get to know you, you have to know yourself.

Think about the following questions.

- What does your school building look like? Are there academic slogans and messages visible? Is academic excellence celebrated and publicized? Are honor rolls and an academic hall of fame visible?
- What is your image as the principal? Are there artifacts that show that you value academic achievement? Are educational books and journals evident? Does your appearance reflect this message? What is in your professional library?
- How do you celebrate success? Do you celebrate individual and group academic success? Are you involved in these academic celebrations? Do building announcements reflect the emphasis on academics?
- How do you spend your time? Do you engage students and staff in academic conversations? Is student work displayed? Do you model reading? Do you model learning?
- Do school publications feature academic work? Does the school website reflect an academic agenda? Do your newsletters and communications to parents reflect your academic agenda?
- Do your faculty meetings have an academic agenda? Is there an academic focus during these meetings? Do you encourage and engage your staff in learning opportunities *(Dalzin)?*

After you settle into your new job, take some time and walk the building using the aforementioned list as a checklist. How many of the boxes can you check?

There are several more rules that you must know. Never forget them.

- *You will always be second guessed.* Your school will be filled with Monday-morning quarterbacks and after-dinner speakers. Some behave that way just to be anti-administration. Some will love to just prove the boss wrong. You can't please everyone, especially these people, so do not try.
- *You will never be visible enough.* No matter how much you work to be out of your office and in classrooms, it will never be good enough. You can help mitigate this by visiting the cafeteria every day and staying a while and also doing hall duty in very

high-profile places. Work to make sure that cantankerous teacher sees you. I used to get really depressed when a teacher, meaning no malice, would come up to me and say, "Hey, I haven't seen you in a while. Where have you been?" That statement crushed me. Be seen, and listen to people. Say a little; listen a lot!

- *You will never communicate well enough for some people.* You can say it, write it, text it, e-mail it, review it time and time again, and still you will have some people claim that you never told them something. Some people tend to have a hard time taking responsibility for themselves. They would rather scapegoat you. You are an easy target. Don't let them get away with it. Put an early end to this behavior as soon as you take over. I had one faculty member who would critique every memo I sent out for grammar and word usage. This person would return my correspondence red-penciled anonymously. It would drive me crazy. They were not trying to help me; they were just trying to make me look bad, and it succeeded. I would have other people proof my work over and over again to help me make sure that this would not happen. I never wanted to give this person the satisfaction of returning it to me. However, they were right. You should never put out sub-quality work. That is why you never write anything in a hurry or when you are upset. Take your time, and do it right without emotion.

Leadership Lessons Learned

- *You must be visible and accessible.*
- *Know what is important to you, and make sure your school tells this story.*
- *Always have an academic agenda.* You must be about student learning and achievement.
- *Say a little. Listen a lot.* Work to develop your good listening skills.
- *Understand that every decision you make will be second guessed.* Get used to it, and make your decisions based on data and what you believe in, not what will please the masses.

"I Want the Truth." "You Can't Handle the Truth"

You probably recognize the above lines spoken by Tom Cruise and Jack Nicholson in the famous courtroom scene in the film *A Few Good Men* (Castle Rock Entertainment). For me this was an extremely powerful scene with both actors at their best. The same concept applies to the people in your school. People will demand that you are open, transparent, and honest. But maybe not to them. And if you are too honest, the masses may be looking to boot you out of the door.

Can a leader be truly open and honest? That is a loaded question! I was taken aback when a good friend and colleague of mine told me that he does not think any school leader can be open and honest. I was a bit shocked inasmuch as I was his principal and later his superintendent for many years and thought of myself as nothing but honest and open. Was he talking about me? Was I included in his broad statement?

Since our conversation, I have not stopped thinking about his comment and began to reexamine my crucial decisions and actions as an educational leader. Who was I?

I did a quick personal survey and found that I believe honesty, integrity, and trust are essential traits for a leader. I thought I possessed all of these qualities. So I started to think about my decisions and how I interacted with people. Although I never thought of myself as a liar, there were times I would spin the truth so much that one may never have recognized it. But if you asked me about myself or if you asked some of the people who worked for me, they would in all likelihood tell you that I was an honest and open leader. They probably viewed me as honest because I most likely told them what they wanted to hear. I was not always true to myself or my beliefs. You can do better.

Overall, people do not want to hear the truth. They want you to tell them what they want to hear. We all need to be stroked to a degree, but does this need blind us from reality? I think it does.

Great leaders have the ability to have crucial conversations in difficult situations, even if the result of the conversation will be negative. These leaders know that to grow, these conversations are essential. These leaders also possess a tireless work ethic and demonstrate this through their approach to the job. Respect and trust are also communicated in what you do, not what you say. That is how people see your true self. These are personal qualities that you either have or you do not have. Some skills can be honed and developed and others cannot.

Leadership Lessons Learned

- *Your actions will speak as to who you are and what you stand for.* People will forget your words but most likely will long remember what you do.
- *Always remain true to yourself.* When you veer off of this course (and at times you will), it will mentally torture you. Veer off of the course too much and then you will not be the person you think you are.

Oops, My Bad!

You will make mistakes. Hopefully you will not make too many mistakes, and of course, hopefully you will not make that fatal mistake that will jeopardize your job. Go slowly when making crucial decisions. Do not cut corners, and know your policies and procedures. I almost made a costly mistake during the first year of my principalship. It would not have been fatal, but it would have been embarrassing. Second, when you do make that mistake, own it. Don't make excuses. Be up front and honest, and put the measures in place that make sure you will not make the same mistake again.

I was a new and enthusiastic principal putting my staff together for a newly restructured school. It was also my first time leading the hiring process, and I was extremely excited about building my team. I thought I prepared quite well inasmuch as I had the entire interview well scripted, I had the right people in the room, we knew our questions (which we labored over developing), and the stage was set. I found my special candidate. It was a great interview. We said goodbye, and as was the practice, I sent my recommendation up to the superintendent for the final piece of the hiring process.

On the night of the board of education meeting to make the appointment official, at around the close of the business day, I received a call from the candidate. He was very cavalier and stated that he had forgotten to tell me something. It seems as though when he was eighteen years old, he was arrested and ultimately pled guilty for possession of marijuana. Although he was able to get his record expunged, he never undertook the process. In my haste to get my recommendation across the finish line, I forgot a key step in the hiring practice. I did not follow district procedures. I hired the candidate off of his resume and was not conscientious in having him fill out the district's application. The application specifically asks questions about arrests. His references checked out beautifully. I was going to have him complete the district's formal application later in the process. I thought he could do it after the meeting. It would have been like post-dating a personal check. No harm, no foul! Everyone did it that way. Right? No, wrong! And remember, this was all taking place hours before the board meeting. Now what was I to do?

I would be lying if I did not share with you that the first thing that ran through my mind was to just let it go. Who would know? Cover it all up and move on! *But always remember that the cover-up is worse than the crime.* This was before the time of sophisticated fingerprint and background checks, and I was sure that everything would be all right. I just knew he would turn out to be a great teacher and a great fit on our new team.

I took a few minutes to clear my head. Then I quickly called the boss and explained to him what had just happened. He was able to pull the recommendation off the hiring agenda without any embarrassing questions. As I was just starting out as a principal of my own building, I did not want to start off in a careless way. My superintendent coached me up, and I never let this happen again. Always remember that the principal is accountable and responsible for everything that happens in the school. It was all my error. I rushed the process. I cut some corners. The employee application clearly asks a question to the candidate seeking information relative to any arrests. Retrospectively, I believe that this candidate would have answered the question honestly. He did not think it was an issue. I did!

Leadership Lessons Learned

- *Know all of your district's policies and procedures and follow them!* Policies are there for a reason. Use them! The same rule applies to all contracts. Know them and follow them!
- *Slow down.* Mistakes are usually made when you hurry or you are totally disorganized. Learn how to manage your deadlines. After this incident, I would never even start an interview without having the completed application before me.
- *The cover-up is always worse than the crime.*

Digging Deeper into Self-Awareness

Leadership Lessons Learned

- *At times you will be given a problem, a job, or an assignment with very little direction, if any.* For me, when I was first hired, I was given a set of keys and pointed in the right direction. Funny, isn't this what we used to do to teachers? We have not made the same progress with new principals and administrators.
- *You must be able to sort out the good and bad that you see.* I can vividly recall watching a veteran principal enjoy and revel in suspending kids. This was not for me.
- *Know that staying in a position too long can burn you out.* Being the sole disciplinarian in a large high school can accelerate this burnout. You can't always be dealing with the negative.
- *Follow your heart and personal vision of your job.* Treat students as you would want them to treat you

- *If you find that the job is not for you, get out.* Do not torment the students or your colleagues. Why did you want this job? If it was for power or money, get out. You are doing an injustice to everyone, including yourself.
- *Think about how students are engaged and taught in the classroom.* Fix that and you will see your discipline problems diminish. I am convinced that all students want a demanding and encouraging teacher.

Commandment 9

Thou Shalt Use the Force to Lead, Yet Always Understand That Some People Prefer the Dark Side.

The Never-Ending Struggle between Good and Evil

This title does sound a bit melodramatic, but I think it encompasses what you need to know. There are constantly two forces at work within your school. One I will refer to as the dark side, and the other I will refer to as the force. Although I am not a huge *Star Wars* fan, it is perhaps the best illustration I can paint for you about the dynamics of the personnel within your school. There is constantly a push of good versus evil. Your staff will ultimately have to pick a side, and I hope for your sake that most of them pick the side of the force. It is up to you to make the force the attractive place to be. I am not suggesting that you throw out all of your standards and allow your school to become a do-your-own-thing type of school. I hope the force becomes such an attractive place in your school that the dark side will shrink away and disappear.

Each person is faced with that precise challenge at some time in his or her career. Does he or she choose the force or the dark side? I do not know exactly when this big challenge will happen. I have heard some colleagues argue that it is the time that tenure is awarded. I don't agree. That is too simple. I believe that some episode happens in either one's professional or personal life that forces him or her to confront this challenge. Your school culture will most likely help him or her decide what side he or she will choose.

Unfortunately, some people will live most of their careers on the dark side. Once a person crosses over to the dark side, it is very hard to bring them back to the force.

Are you a walnut tree or a marigold? That sounds like an odd question. However, I think once I explain that question, you will see the importance of this distinction. Jennifer Gonzalez in one of her frequent blogs wrote a powerful article entitled, "Find Your Marigold: One Essential Rule for New Teachers," where she eloquently warns new teachers that there are many walnut tress (other teachers) planted within your school. Gonzalez reminds us that anything that is planted near a walnut tree ultimately dies. Walnut trees act as a sort of poison, whereas marigolds will improve the quality of life for any plant that grows near them. Gardeners actually plant these flowers around other plants to help them grow. They somehow support and nurture existing plants. Your school also has teacher marigolds. It must be your goal to have more marigolds than walnut trees. Walnut trees grow on the dark side, and marigolds exist in the force. Marigolds make your school and the people within the school stronger. Walnut trees will weaken and destroy your school. Make sure your new people are always paired with and near a marigold. That is the lesson to be learned in this story. It just makes sense *(Gonzalez)*.

Leadership Lessons Learned

- *Walnut trees poison. Marigolds nurture.* Make sure your school is full of marigolds.
- *Everyone at some point is confronted with the choice of going to the dark side.* It is up to you to make that choice a no-brainer. The force must win!

Bitter until the Very End

I have seen this routine time and time again. A person retires after a long career, and his or her departure is just filled with bitterness. The person is well respected and has been promoted several times during his or her career. He or she is leaving with a great pension and some great memories. So, why is he or she so angry? Somehow in a school most people leave bitter about something.

I recall a situation where a principal was seeking the vacant superintendent's position. On the surface this person was qualified for the position. At times I valued this person's opinion and guidance. Yet, like most of us, this person was driven and wanted a chance at the top spot. The interview process went favorably for this person, and he or she was one of the three finalists for the position. The other finalists included a dark horse internal candidate and an outside candidate.

As the selection process unfolded, the candidate learned that the person from outside of the district was the recommendation. Few people, if any, gave the other internal candidate a chance. The outside person accepted the position. Both internal candidates were disappointed.

As luck would have it, there was a public board meeting within the next few days to finalize the deal. One of the dejected candidates attended the board meeting and delivered a passionate yet blistering speech lamenting the board's choice for the new superintendent. There was clearly a feeling of entitlement for this position. I viewed this address to the board as a full-fledged attack.

I understood what had happened. Often, the board will feel compelled to bring in an outside candidate to infuse new ideas and be that change agent for the district. There is nothing wrong with the internal candidates; there is just this drive to seek a fresh start.

As fate would have it, within a couple of days, the outside candidate withdrew his acceptance of the position. The board was now scrambling. What was the board to do? For them it was really simple. They appointed the third-place dark horse candidate, who ultimately held the position for just about a decade.

If the disappointed internal candidate had just kept quiet, I believe that this person would have gotten the job. It would have been a natural fallback selection.

The person stayed in the district for a few more years and in my opinion became more and more bitter and angry as each year passed.

Leadership Lessons Learned

- *Keep your mouth shut.* Of course, you may be disappointed, but just dust yourself off and move forward. Yesterday is ancient history.
- *Nothing is owed you. No one is entitled to anything!* Do your job. The district owes you a paycheck. Promotions and positions do not always go to the most qualified.
- *Self-pity is a wasted emotion.* Quit feeling sorry for yourself, and get on with your career.

There Is No Honor among Thieves

Some people just cannot help themselves. They are willing to throw everything away in a matter of moments. I wonder what possesses people to behave in this way. Is the pull from the dark side that strong?

A school is a prime market for thieves. People are usually trustworthy and are usually careless. Doors are left unlocked, and supplies and equipment tend to be left out in the open. Pocketbooks are left on top of desks or are visible in unlocked drawers. I had always considered the school just like a home. You don't steal from family. You don't steal from teammates, and you don't steal from colleagues. You just don't steal! In these environments, one hopes that the feeling of trust supersedes any feelings of getting rich quick or beating the system.

We had a terrible practice of receiving orders during the summer. We knew that the practice was bad, talked about it frequently, yet never did anything about it. Truckers dropped supplies off into the cafeteria, where they sat until the spirit moved our custodial staff to store them more securely.

There were countless times that I entered the building and would say to myself that this situation was an incident waiting to happen. I would note this but then would get caught up in the day and forget to do something about it. You see we always did it this way. How many times have you failed to change something because of that statement? And how many times did you live to regret it?

We received our order of computers, and they sat in the cafeteria for days. And by the time we got around to storing them properly, some were missing.

The first thing we did was to search the building and question all custodians to see if they moved them to a secure storeroom and just forgot about them. When that failed to produce the missing laptops, we went to the videotape. It is important to note that the student cafeteria, where the shipment was dropped, was fully covered with video surveillance. I strongly encourage you to make sure your student cafeteria has video camera coverage. This will help you avoid problems if a large student incident ever occurs. The cafeteria is a prime place for a protest, a physical altercation, or dare I say a food fight of some sort, and you will need some proof when it is time to mete out punishment. All students and staff knew that the cafeteria was on camera. This was no secret. I wanted everyone to know that their actions would always be monitored and recorded. While watching the video, it was easy to see the culprit. One of our veteran custodians made two trips out to the Dumpster after dropping boxes of laptops in the trash barrel. On the way to the Dumpster, this individual stopped at his car to unload the booty. For me it was a bit sad because I always felt that the person was a trustworthy and very likeable individual. When I interviewed this person and shared the video, he readily admitted it. I felt our conversation was enlightening. This person explained to me that he walked by the boxes for days and it seemed that as each day progressed, the boxes were calling. This made me wonder that if these boxes were talking to him, why didn't they just tell him to lock them up? There came a point in time where the temptation became too great and so the boxes were removed. Yes, this person was remorseful, yet this person paid deeply for this act. The thief was fired from the job and ultimately had to answer the charges in superior court. A job for life with full benefits and a pension plan was thrown away for several hundred dollars' worth of computers. A truly sad case.

Another time I had to deal with a custodian who figured out a way to break into our vault in the main office. Never thinking we would catch the person, we set up a very obvious and inexpensive camera focusing on the vault doorway. This person was so careless that as this individual entered the vault, the camera was bumped, and this person actually adjusted it. I thanked this person for giving us a better view. Just like the previous case, the drive and intent to steal several dollars cost the culprit a great deal more.

Leadership Lessons Learned

- *Be extremely careful who you trust*
- *Never leave anything of value out in plain sight.*
- *Closely monitor fundraisers, ticket sales, and cafeteria money.* Although not directly on point for this scenario, these areas, because of slipshod practices, are prime areas for theft. People see this as easy money. Make sure tickets are numbered and recorded. Although you may not be directly involved, *you are responsible!*

Cheaters Never Prosper. Or Do They?

This old proverb tells us tons about life. Any short-term gain is just not worth it. Consequences will be painful. Never delude yourself. If you cheat, you will be caught.

I know the few times I had to deal with alleged cheating, the person was usually quite surprised that what he or she was accused of doing was actually cheating. I always wondered if they really believed this, or did they somehow trick themselves into believing it? Who knows.

I also understand that sometimes the situation drives us to cut corners. I think we have done this with the renewed emphasis on standardized tests. Everyone is pressured for their students to perform. This pressure comes from both external and internal forces. Some people are driven to cheat because of the pressure they place upon themselves. Others are driven to cheat because of the pressure others put upon them.

I think in the following scenarios, you will see a combination of both forces at work. I know, as the principal and superintendent, I put pressure on people to have high test scores. I am a competitor, and I should have known that not all people share my drive or spirit. I would try to make most things a competition. I would talk to teachers about why their test scores were not the best in their grade level. I wanted to know why their students were not performing better. Perhaps it was just the perfect storm. Maybe it was the confluence of the teacher's personal drive, my competitive spirit, and the pressure from the state and the newly imposed teacher evaluation systems. I warn all principals to be very cognizant of the pressure they may apply to teachers because not everyone will respond the way you intended. However, I will not take the responsibility for any person cheating. Regardless of any external forces, they clearly knew what they were doing. They clearly knew right from wrong. It was the teacher who crossed the line, not me.

I had to navigate two separate teacher cheating issues, and in both cases, the cheating was similar. Both teachers took a great deal of pride in their work and their students' performance. I would consider both teachers to be good teachers who enjoyed a quality reputation in the school and in the parental community. Parents could not wait for their child to have one of these teachers. (Perhaps it was because their child's test scores improved?)

In one case, the teacher dealt with mostly special needs children. It turned out that these students were outperforming the best and brightest students in the building. I can recall studying the test results, and they jumped off of the page. When I dug a little deeper, I found that this was not an isolated year. Students continually performed beyond their ability. When they left this teacher, their scores returned to what one would expect.

In the second case, the class showed a bit of an anomaly but nothing crazy. Other teachers began to turn this person in to the administration when they heard the students talking about the test procedures in this class. I think personalities in this case started to get in the way, and other adults were anxious to see this teacher fall in some way. I can only speculate as to the reason, but at the end of the day, the reasons are not important.

In the first case, I contacted the state and described what I saw in the tests, and they started an investigation. Let me assure you that you do not want the state breathing down your back, but it is always better when you report an issue. I followed the same procedure in the subsequent case. And always remember, the state always wants to catch a big fish, namely a principal or superintendent. It is your head that they want as a trophy. That is why it is always essential that you cross every t and dot every i. Do not miss a deadline, read every memo, and attend every training session offered.

It turns out that both teachers provided too much guidance and help to the students on test day. They crossed the line. They used body language, voice inflections, and other mnemonics to guide the children. The students were well coached, knowing what these signals meant. Although I do not believe this was overt, the students got it. In both cases, the teachers stretched the rules, and just like a rubber band, when stretched too far, it broke. They crossed a line that they had blurred. At the end of the day, they knew better. They cheated.

It was career altering or ending for both of them. It also impacted the principal who was in charge of test administration because this person was careless. The principal took too much for granted. Although the principal's career was not ended, it was certainly damaged.

Leadership Lessons Learned

- *Never take anything for granted.* I was almost tricked into thinking, *Not this teacher* or *This person would never cheat.* No matter how much it may hurt, you must never lose focus. Know that anyone is capable of anything.
- *State officials want the biggest trophy possible.* Although they will take the teacher, they want your head on the wall.
- *If you see a problem, report it!* Believe me, when I first saw the test anomaly, I thought of just burying it. No one would ever find

out. There are those magic words you should never use. They will destroy you. People may forgive some honest mistakes. They will never forgive the cover-up or lie.

- *Do not be careless and take things for granted.* Follow the directions you were given. Follow them exactly.

Digging Deeper into the Dark Side and the Force

Leadership Lessons Learned

- *At times you will let personalities get in your way.* You will let destructive behavior continue because of your friendship with a person. When you do this, students and teachers are negatively impacted. I let a "friend" kill my high school library. Students and staff were not welcome. The librarian, my long-time friend, had to go. What was the matter with me? I let the dark side win. I needed a kick in the butt. You need a trusted confidante to do this kicking. I always put some salve on the issue but never solved it.
- *You cannot allow friendships to get in the way of running the school*
- *When you have a superstar on your team, you cannot let them leave.* Try to design a job around them to best nurture them and to help them grow. *Think outside of the box.* Never underestimate that by allowing this person to leave you can drastically negatively impact the culture and the climate of your school.

Commandment 10

Thou Shalt Know Thy Job. Are Thou an Operations Manager, or an Instructional Leader?

You Are the Principal—Now Lead!

For years, I always wondered that as the principal, was I an operations manager or an instructional leader? Believe it or not, this question, and yes, this frustration would keep me up at night. I always thought of myself as an educator. I wanted to focus on teaching and learning.

I quickly found out that on most days, I was the building's operations manager. I had to concern myself with things like leaky toilets and faulty bus schedules. Although on the surface these jobs have little to do with teaching and learning, issues such as these greatly impact the school. If you cannot get operations right, you might as well forget about teaching and learning. It would be nice if your school had two distinct people to handle these roles, but that is not a reality for most schools. Your job will at many times will seem like that of a triage nurse, prioritizing who or what is most in need of your services. You will be the maintenance director, policeman, babysitter, referee, or social worker and at the same time be that instructional leader. At the secondary level, you will spend most of your day as the disciplinarian. That can get old very quickly. It can also burn you out. My office very quickly became the place where you could dump your problems. People are masters at the dump-and-run technique. And I was the master at letting them do this.

I began to look at ways that I could lead various personal educational initiatives. I began to focus on topics such as the minority achievement gap, leadership issues, socioeconomic issues, and how to market our school in a more positive light. Forcing myself to spend some time on these issues on a daily basis kept me focused on education.

Many times, operation management turned quickly into crisis management. The principal can very quickly become a great crisis manager, while simultaneously becoming a marginal instructional leader. And take my word for it—you will first be judged as to how you deal with these crises.

Leadership Lessons Learned

- *Operations management and instructional leadership are inextricably linked.*
- *You can forget about climate, culture, and learning if your operations are a mess.* You have to take care of quality-of-life issues before you can think about instructional issues.

Tell People What You Want, and Then Hold Them Accountable!

Be explicit, concise, and direct. It sounds so simple, yet why did it take me so long to realize this? I think for the most part, I took for granted that people knew what I wanted. I took for granted that people would use common sense when conducting business. I assumed way too much. Assume nothing!

Some of my most rewarding time as a principal was spent participating as part of my quasi site-based management team. We called this group the action team. The action team was made up of a group of teachers, administrators, parents, community members, and if possible, a board of education member. This was a very structured group with many set procedures

This group allowed for the participation of many people to determine the way the school operated. It was a powerful group, and it helped make me a good participatory leader. Let me caution you—being a participatory leader is hard work. I think it is much easier to be that autocrat staying sequestered in the corner office. That method may be easier, but it is not nearly as effective. To make a long story short, the action team got things done and was held accountable by the rest of the school. We attempted to manage the school through building consensus. Very few decisions or discussions were off limits. (We never talked personnel.) Problems were solved, procedures developed, and initiatives started or stopped by consensus, not a vote.

I can vividly recall one day when I got into a very heated exchange with a team member whom I both liked and respected. We have become lifelong friends, and we still talk teaching and learning today. The source of our argument was that I was lamenting how disappointed I was that our teachers were having such a hard time doing what I thought were simple tasks. These tasks included taking attendance in homeroom, sending a student to the nurse, or filling out specific forms—tasks that I thought should be completed by just using common sense.

My colleague argued that I was the cause of this problem because I never told people how to do these tasks. I admit that I took it for granted that a high school teacher could do these things. He argued that teachers wanted to do these things correctly, but because they were never told how to do these things, they remained lost.

I finally relented and designed a framework for handling homeroom duty. I was amazed at how it worked. My trusted colleague was correct. I was wrong because I took too much for granted. As a result of this, I designed a small book I entitled *Frameworks and Rubrics*. I tried to think of everything that needed to be done in my school and wrote a framework as to how to handle it. Topics ranged from seeking supplies to sending a child to the office. I was amazed how this worked. I was never clear to the staff about my expectations. Finally, people started to give me what I wanted. The lesson here is simple. Tell people what you want, show them how to do it, coach them on the topic, and then hold them accountable. So, grab your action team (if you don't have one, start one), and begin working on a similar book. You will be surprised by how well it works.

Leadership Lessons Learned

- *Explain to your staff what you expect, show them how to do it, coach them, and hold them accountable.*
- *Be careful about taking prior knowledge for granted.* People come to your school with many different ways of doing things. Teach them your school's way.
- *Widely communicate your expected practices and procedures.*
- *Understand that being a participatory leader is hard work, but it is worth it.*

Enough Already—Please Stop Boring Me to Death!

I must plead guilty to this one. I have bored many of my staff to death. I love meetings. I am sure that I am in the very small percentage of people who enjoy these encounters. And as I reflect upon many of the meetings I had control of, my participants had a hard time staying engaged. I knew this and worked hard at it, but I still lost people along the way. But I must stop here and admonish everyone. Each participant has a personal responsibility to make a meeting worthwhile. To get something out of a meeting, one must contribute.

I also know of many people who will look for creative ways to escape meetings. A valued colleague of mine once told me that every meeting must have a clearly defined agenda and start and stop on time. If you can follow that simple two-step framework, you will be ahead of the game. But can you follow that simple framework?

Do you really need the meeting? And if you do, does everyone have access to it, and do they have the agenda beforehand? Is there another way you can distribute information? For me, I would always include a time period where we could talk about learning. With all of the other minutia floating around, sometimes we would forget our true purpose, and for me that was to improve learning.

Never forget the unofficial group social norm; you are not to ask questions or needlessly prolong the discussion because we want to get out of here. I am sure you have been in a similar group situation, perhaps in your superintendent's meeting. The people who contribute to the discussion are never viewed favorably by their colleagues. Isn't that unfortunate? This mindset about meetings speaks volumes about the culture of your school.

It is therefore imperative that when you do meet as a group, it is well planned and thought out. I strongly suggest that you practice your facilitation skills before the meeting and understand what points in the meeting where there could be dissent, questions, discussion, or any other perhaps unforeseen reaction. I can recall being so busy that I waited for the last minute to create my agenda and was running out of my office door with the ink still not dry on the pages. I know in these meetings very little was accomplished. By the same token, these types of meetings destroyed whatever credibility I had built up with my staff regarding the worth and importance of my meetings. In essence, these meetings did more harm than good.

People will disengage when nothing is offered to them intellectually. They will also disengage if they believe their other work is more important to them, on both the personal or professional level. If given a choice, most teachers would rather stay in their classrooms checking off items on their own personal to-do list than sit in a needless meeting. Never underestimate the importance of how you spend another person's time.

Do not try to tap dance through the meetings. Everyone will know that you did not do your homework.

There is an art of building an agenda, especially if you want to accomplish your goals. You may also have to limit the number of things you want to accomplish at a meeting. Sometimes it might be just one important item. Some groups cannot handle more than one important item on an agenda. It is important that you plan your meetings to get some final decisions made. Do not overwhelm or overstimulate your participants. There were times when I would backload the very important items on an agenda because I knew at that time, I could push through my point of view and get to consensus quickly because people wanted to get out of the meeting.

It is also very important that every person in the meeting understand the rules for the meeting. Newcomers must be coached in this area. You will soon find out how the chemistry of your group can change with one new participant. Group dynamics are sensitive and ever changing. This is another reason that we take the time necessary to onboard new participants. It is also important that even if your group is running quite smoothly, your protocols and procedures should be reviewed.

Whenever meetings are held, especially ones where the participants are vested and passionate, conflict can be expected. How will you deal with this conflict? It is important that dissent happens and is aired, but it can never denigrate into personal attacks that are disrespectful and damaging. Allowing this to take place will destroy the meeting and the hopes of ever reaching a decision. It also could damage future relationships.

When you are leading the meeting, *lead*! It is easy for someone to hijack the meeting. Some may be vocal and overt in this process, but others can be sly and manipulative and can destroy a meeting covertly. By preplanning, you should know the agenda and the purpose of each agenda item thoroughly. Do not allow your leadership to be undermined. Remember, it is your meeting. Yes, discussion, dissent, and hearing from everyone is important, but you can never lose control.

It is critically important that as a leader, you keep your emotions in check. I wish I could have always practiced what I preach here. When I lost my patience or became emotional, I ended up sabotaging my own meeting. Some on your team might be experts at pressing the right button for you to lose your patience. Be smarter than your participants. Do not let them push your personal hot button.

It is critical that you maintain energy at the meeting. Sometimes the air gets depleted from the room. Eyes start to droop, and some may be sleeping with their eyes open. You may feel your energy dwindling. It is time for a break. Get some air, stretch your legs, come back, and refocus. Your energy will in turn dictate the energy of the group. If you are not passionate and enthused, how can you expect others to share the same energy level?

Take some time to reflect and evaluate on how the meeting went. This can be done with a small group of trusted colleagues who can honestly and candidly talk to you. Be smart, accept their feedback, and do not take it personally. Reflect and professionally grow as a result of this feedback.

I have always been disappointed when I watched people enter the room with their body language communicating a negative demeanor. It is written all over their faces that they do not want to be there. This negativity drains the energy from the room before the meeting begins. Just think of the impression one's negative attitude has on the facilitator when he or she is looking at pouting and disengaged faces. Each participant must choose his or her own personal attitude of engagement and excitement for the meeting.

Arriving for the meeting promptly is critical. Nothing is more annoying for the facilitator or the entire group than when participants trickle in. This especially goes for the leader. Do not keep people waiting. This is both rude and disrespectful.

I used to be able to regularly predict those who would be late. When you are attending a meeting, take careful note of traffic patterns to the meeting location. Always be prepared for those parking lot meetings that are apt to happen. A real irritant for me would be for a person to walk in late, carrying a designer cup of coffee. This communicated to me that the person could stop for a coffee, yet could not be on time for the meeting. When I addressed this, the tardy participant wondered why it was such a big deal. This attitude was disappointing at best, and it just fueled a negative culture.

Please keep your cell phones tucked away. Nothing is worse than looking out at the group and seeing everyone reading their e-mail or texting. Take care of impending questions from your home base before you attend the meeting. For example, a meeting should not have to be interrupted so your secretary can ask you if the students are to go outside for recess on that day. This decision should have been made ahead of time. I am also aware that people would text each other in the meeting—yes criticizing me and my meeting, while I was leading the meeting.

People get tired of the meeting bully. These bullies tend to hijack every meeting and are strategic passive-aggressive manipulators. There are only so many ways one can say no. I also knew a person who felt that if he yelled the loudest, he would win his point of contention. It was immature, but for him it proved effective because he was allowed to bully.

Side conversations are also quite annoying and distracting. Save your comments to your colleague until a break or after the meeting. If several side conversations are going on at one time, the important message will surely be lost.

Just remember, you will be judged along every step of the way. A meeting can very easily make or break you.

Leadership Lessons Learned

- *Meetings must be organized and skillfully facilitated with an agenda and a starting and ending time.*
- *People must be allowed to discuss and dissent.* The meeting cannot be about you.
- *Practice your facilitation skills.*
- *When it is your meeting, control it.*
- *Know exactly what you want to accomplish.* If necessary, limit what you put on the agenda.
- *As the leader in the meeting, you must keep your emotions in check.*
- *Read the energy level in a meeting.* Work to keep the distracting behaviors of the participants to a minimum. Put all electronics away. Know when it is time to take a break.
- *Expect promptness from the participants.* You must be there well ahead of time, with everything set up and working. There is

nothing worse than having a technical problem during the meeting. Test everything. Kick off the meeting on time.

- *Evaluate the meeting.* Have some colleagues tell you the truth about how the meeting went. Make sure they are honest. Do not let your feelings get hurt. To improve, you have to know the truth.

Action, Action, I Want Action!

My experience tells me that principals are experts at giving lip service. We like to hear ourselves talk. It is dreadful when you put us all in the same room with one microphone. We will fight with each other to get a hold of that mic. However, if you want to improve student learning, improve teaching, and improve the overall culture of the school, you need less talk and more action.

I am sure every administrator is involved somehow with short, frequent visits into a classroom. Some administrators will arrive in a classroom as a group. The designed purpose of these visits is to see good teaching and to get an overall view as to what is happening in the classroom. Of equal importance for these walks is to make focused recommendations to improve instruction. Each district probably has its own set of things that administrators are looking for. But what happens after the visit? It is here that I will argue that the principal gives his or her best lip service to the situation. Principals come and visit and maybe say a nice thing or two to the teacher. But what else happens? What should happen?

I know that some principals will send a quick note to the teacher, usually praising something they saw. Both the principal and the teacher feel good about themselves. However, nothing positive happened to improve instruction or for that matter, student learning.

When I became a superintendent, I would argue with my principals that it was not about the visit but the conversation you have with the teacher after the visit. One day, one of my principals stood up and told me that it must include so much more. He argued that it can't be about the walk itself or the follow-up talk. The result of the visit must be the teacher's action that occurred as a result of your visit. This made a great deal of sense to me.

Every time you conduct a classroom visit, it is incumbent upon you to talk with that teacher and share what you saw and what you would like to see. And then, on your next walkthrough, see if any of the actions you suggested have been implemented. This is where you have to be the coach. I believe strongly that this is the only way to help teachers improve instruction. But of course, unless you embark on an honest discussion, your assessment will never have the impact it should have had. But once again, another question arises. Do you have the relationship with that teacher to enter into this type of honest dialog?

Leadership Lessons Learned

- *You talk too much!* Learning walks are not about the walk or the talk. They are about the teacher action that occurs as a result of your visit and conversation.
- *Give the teacher small things to work on that you will look for on your next visit.* Be prepared to enter into a discussion to see if the results were what you had hoped for.

Digging Deeper into Knowing Your Job

Leadership Lessons Learned

- *There will be times when you will be called upon to clean up other people's messes, both physical and emotional. Just do it!*
  - One day early in my administrative career, I got called to the bus to take a fire ax away from one of my bus drivers as he waved it at my students. Of course, my students were not being cooperative and he could not take it anymore, so he brandished the fire ax at the students. I was able to diffuse the situation and return the dismissal to normalcy.
  - There were times when I would call my wife to bring me a clean shirt because it became bloodstained breaking up a

student fight. I never realized how this troubled my wife. To me, it was no big deal. It was part of the job. Remember that *school administration is a family commitment.*

o I had to physically intervene when a parent decided to "whoop" his child in school. Both the father and son were bigger than me, and it was an adventure. I had to protect my student, and I did it.

- *You cannot lose your emotional control.* You must be the adult in a world of childishness. Many times, the childlike behavior will come from the adults you work with. I had to apply this theory to a colleague of mine when we were engaged in a heated discussion and he replied to a request of mine that if I wanted a guarantee, I should go buy a toaster. Needless to say, I had to call upon all of my resources not to punch him in the nose. I had to be the adult. I am glad I was able to do that.

Afterword
They Shoot Horses, Don't They? Everyone Has A Shelf Life!

They Shoot Horses, Don't They?

Just like that stale loaf of bread that sits on the grocery shelf too long, understand that you, too, have a shelf life. You have an expiration date.

You will eventually tire. Maybe you lose a step in your speed to respond. Maybe you are challenged by a younger, more fit leader. Maybe people are tired of hearing your voice. Maybe you are not up to the daily challenge any longer. You become both physically and emotionally drained. You are not the leader you once were. If you know it and feel it, so will others. I never wanted to leave by being chased out. I never wanted to leave on a stretcher, and I never wanted to leave by taking pills to settle myself. Sadly, I have seen colleagues leave in the aforementioned states, only to quickly wither in their retirement.

The same thing happens in other professions. When you stay too long, people tend to stop listening. They turn your message off. In athletics, head coaches and managers can only stay in one place so long. Your message loses its appeal. Perhaps you too have lost some of that emotion and passion that you once had. It is impossible to maintain the intensity level needed to thrive for an endless amount of time. The key for me is recognizing the fact that you do have a shelf life. Your professional time runs out. In a sense, just like that loaf of bread on the shelf of your grocery store, you have an expiration date. Embrace this concept. Be aware of it when you see it coming, and I assure you that you will see it and you will sense it. Once this happens, you need to create and plan your exit strategy to go out on top. For me, that is the only way to go. You have earned it. Do not wait to be chased out of the door because if you hang around well after your expiration date, you will be chased out, and it will not be pretty.

Once you have decided to leave, it is time to celebrate and exult. You might not have always been successful, but you contributed. You have had the opportunity to touch many people in a positive way.

Everyone always told me, "You will know when this day comes." I always asked, "How will I know?" No matter whom I spoke with, their answer remained simple and consistent: "You will just know!" To a degree, they were right. However, I always worry about those who choose to stay too long. They do not know that their time is up, and their final years on the job become torture. It becomes painful for everyone, including yourself. It will eat away at each person differently. There is a time when no matter who you are, your skills will erode.

What if all the signs and signals tell you that you are ready to go, but you are unable to retire because of your age or financial situation? What if you are five years away from this magical date? Ten years? What if retirement is all you are thinking about? If this is the case, you must do a serious lifetime assessment and seek to make some changes in your personal and professional life. You cannot stay where you are miserable. You cannot become that walnut tree.

You may need to change districts. You may need to change schools. You may need to change positions. You cannot keep doing the same thing every day because now you are cheating your staff, your students, and perhaps more importantly, yourself. Make sure the change is your idea. I know I have moved people administratively because they were no longer effective in their roles. I sometimes had to create a position for them. And perhaps the most difficult thing was convincing them that they should embrace the move. I know I had some people convince themselves that they were being promoted, when in fact they were being removed from the front lines. I let them believe what they wanted to believe so they could make it through the day. Yet I think that at night, when they were alone and peaceful with their inner thoughts, they knew they were being replaced because they could no longer perform. Making these moves was the right thing for the school and district. You cannot impede progress, and you cannot, even if it is inadvertent, hurt the children. The adults in the schools have done this for too long. I know that the next generation of principals will be better at this.

If you stay too long, people will forget all of the happiness and good things you accomplished. They will forget all of your great wins and only remember the losses. Do not become an embarrassment to yourself.

Do not become the principal who teachers love to work for you because you have become a pushover. Do not allow yourself to become that principal who teachers and students see as now too miserable, too nasty, and too mean. You may have forgotten why you became a teacher or a principal in the first place. It is very easy to become the joke that your colleagues talk about in the faculty room or the principal who is lampooned as a caricature of a school leader.

When we slip and stay too long, we are negatively impacting the lives and futures of a generation of students. To me, that is a crime!

I can remember when I was many years away from retirement and longingly talking about this with my father. I was just like him, a workaholic. I was married to my district, and he was married to General Motors. And just like him, although we both did quite well in our careers, sacrifices had to be made at home. As I was relishing the thought of retirement, which for me was still many years away, my father stepped up and told me that when he retired, it was the worst day in his life. On this day, he became a nobody. To me, that was a profound statement that made me sad and stayed with me for the duration of my career. It still resonates with me today. He allowed his job to define him. It is hard not to become your job. When you are asked, perhaps at a workshop, to talk about yourself, I bet that you start out by saying that you are a principal. This is not who you are. It is what you do! My father never understood this. I think that right up to the day he died, he would have started to talk about his role in General Motors. I think he missed something. When it is time, embrace your retirement. You have only completed one leg of your race or one part of your game. Your journey is far from over.

References

Dalzin, V. (2010). Cultivating an Academic Image. *Principal Leadership,* v10(6). 64–66.

Fried, R. L. (2005). *The Game of School: We all play it, how it hurts kids and what it will take to change it.* San Francisco: Jossey-Bass.

Gonzalez, J. (2013). Find Your Marigold: The One Essential Rile for New Teachers. Retrieved from https://www.cultofpedagogy.com/marigolds/.

Waters, R. (2014). *The Evolution of Teaching.* Maryland: Rowman and Litttlefield.

About the Author

Edward Yergalonis served for thirty-eight years in public education, most of those years in administration. In addition to being a teacher and a coach, he has served as an assistant principal, principal of a middle school, principal of a high school, and an assistant superintendent, finally retiring as the superintendent of the Rahway Public Schools, in Rahway, New Jersey. He holds degrees from the College of William and Mary and the University of Cincinnati. He has widely presented and is the author of articles mostly focusing on leadership. He has served on the National Urban Task Force for the National Association of Secondary School Principals and the College Scholarship Service Assembly for the College Board. His first book, *EduKate Me—a Survival Guide for All New School Employees, Unspoken Rules for Working in a School* is a valuable guide to help all new school employees find success. He currently serves as a mentor to new principals and writes a weekly blog focusing on educational leadership that can be found at www.expectingexcellence.net.

Acknowledgments

Mrs. Mary Yergalonis, my wife, for serving as my personal copy editor and biggest supporter.

Mrs. Tiffany Lynch-Beer for preventing me from butchering the English language.

Ms. Erin Marie Kelly for serving as my editorial consultant.

Dr. Richard Waters, a trusted advisor and friend, for his input and guidance in the completion of this work.

Kudos to all of the teachers, administrators, support staff, parents, and students I have worked with over the years. It has been my pleasure to serve. You have made the journey extremely worthwhile.